I

May you continue to
paint your own life in
excellence!

With much love,

Aimie Wren.

April 2014.

A Lady,
Her Letters,
Our Legacy

A Lady, Her Letters, Our Legacy

Hand Painted

Aime Wren

Library of Congress Control Number: 2014903976
ISBN: Hardcover   978-1-4931-7877-3
                 Softcover   978-1-4931-7878-0
                 eBook   978-1-4931-7876-6

This book was printed in the United States of America.

Rev. date: 04/09/2014

To order additional copies of this book, contact:
Xlibris LLC
1-888-795-4274
www.Xlibris.com
Orders@Xlibris.com
550247

For my gentle and gracious grandmother, who wore her silver hair teased and swirled up in a majestic French roll, who comforted me when I cried, and who herself as a child won all the spelling bees in her village school but could not continue her education. Like many girls in her era, after completing grade seven, she was needed to help with work at home on the farm.

To my sister, whose intelligence and humor far outshone mine and whose strength of character has been tested deeply both in childhood and in adult life. My sister whose overcoming spirit is triumphant and whose laughter I share.

For my beautiful daughter, so that she will read of resilience and find gracious examples of purpose and strength.

And to the lady whose life broke my silence.

Thou makest the outgoing of the morning and the evening to rejoice.

—Psalm 65:8, KJV

Get up early and go to the mountain, and watch God make a morning. The dull grey will give way as God pushes the sun towards the horizon, and there will be tints and hues of every shade, that will blend into one perfect light as the full-orbed sun bursts into view. As the King of day moves forth majestically, flooding the earth and every lowly vale, listen to the music of Heaven's choir as it sings the majesty of God and the glory of the morning.

—Streams in the Desert,
Mrs. Charles E. Cowman

The twelve gates were twelve pearls, each gate made of a single pearl. The great street of the city was pure gold, like transparent glass.

—Revelation 21:21, NIV

Contents

Acknowledgements   11

Part 1 Letters

E-Mail Letters Between Abigail and Jenya   13

Part 2 Seven Colour Lessons

Hawthorne Yellow   71

Navy Blue   75

Scarlet Red   85

Lilac Mauve   91

Flagstone Gray   97

Velvet Peach   103

Robin's Egg Aqua   109

Part 3 Life from the Studio

Pearl White: the Mixing Colour of Peace   137

The United Nations Declaration of the Rights of the Child   139

Acknowledgements

With special thanks to Beth Williams. For her intelligent, gracious, and outstanding mentoring. My heartfelt gratitude and appreciation always.

To Martha for her brilliant consistency, to Wendy, for her cheerful love. To Susan for her refined companionship. To Laura for her spiritual intelligence, to Olivia whom I first entrusted with the colours. To Charmaine, who prayerfully encouraged me forward. To Ange who envisioned the name. To Liza, who's example of endurance I value.

And to Dr. Kate Henry, whose professional graciousness is grounded, and sincere

From: Abigail <Abigail@sympatico.ca>
Subject: On the Same Page
Date: 9 March 2011, 5:46:09 PM EST
To: Jenya <Jenya@hotmail.com>

Dear Jenya,

Amazon could not send Xinran, but Indigo did. Oh my goodness . . .
I heard their *Hidden Voices* and could not stop listening to every
tragic page. She writes with direct simplicity. Stories that carry such
heavy weight—each suppressed girl story screams itself so immensely
that I felt my very own braids being cut off. Oh, Jenya, her next one,
Sky Burial, is sitting on top of my book pile. The small hardcover is
requiring my complete willpower to save closed for March break. If it
wasn't for the boys' hockey playoffs, I'd give in to the temptation to
read it, and maybe even so I will!

I hope your day is wonderful, and that you have time to live in the best
of pages.

Much love,
Abigail

From: Jenya <Jenya@hotmail.com>
Subject: Dance
Date: 14 March 2011, 7:50 AM
To: Abigail <Abigail@sympatico.ca>

Certainly not a Brethren boy on the dance floor (footage from
Charles's South African trip).

Jx

From: Abigail <Abigail@sympatico.ca>
Subject: Re: Dance
Date: 21 March 2011, 5:40:56 PM EDT
To: Jenya <Jenya@hotmail.com>

Dear Jenya,

The video from South Africa looks great! I got your e-mail on my iPhone while in Florida but was able to download and watch it on my laptop today. The children are so sweet; the elephants, large; safari landscape, beautiful. And Charles dancing . . . he's having *so* much fun. What a great opportunity for him and his friends! The previous generation of Brethren boys missed out on so much, didn't they?

Since flying in from Orlando, I attended my very first gallery show. It was a display of six of my humble paintings, along with other students' work and professional artists'—a culmination of three years of lessons celebrated with friends, well-wishers, even some hockey parents, as well as my father and sister's surprise visit.

This was all on the night right after I flew in from Orlando and the day before William's team won the gold medal on the hockey game for OMHA, keeping up with his brother who had won the same tournament for his age-group the weekend before. This is a record year as I don't believe that both of the boys' teams will make it that far again in the same hockey season. Winning gold at this level is as high as they can go. They are tired but thrilled. Maybe their hard work during practice paid off!

The Florida sunshine was equaled in excitement by the rental convertible, the sight of three teenage girls taking in Disney music and lights at night, buying wedge ribbon shoes, and palm trees towering green in the cloudless royal blue sky. There is nothing like hot sunshine mid-Canadian March. The trip was a greatly appreciated highlight between the hockey arenas.

I hope that your days are flowing well, that you get to dine on the finest sushi from time to time and that you are feeling encouraged along the way.

XOXO,
Abigail

From: Jenya <Jenya@hotmail.com>
Subject: Sunshine
Date: 23 March 2011, 9:13 AM
To: Abigail <Abigail@sympatico.ca>

Hi, Abigail,

Glad you had a fun time in Florida. I hear the weather was great. Don't think my in-laws are thinking of returning for a while with wintery conditions back home.

Congratulations on your first gallery show! How sweet of your dad and sister to surprise you. I'd love to see your art, maybe in the summer!

Congratulations to the boys on their great achievements. You must all be so excited and proud.

It's been another crazy week. Charles Jr. just returned from a Model United Nations conference in Shanghai, my helper took off for her daughter's graduation for ten days, Charles left a few days ago for Sydney . . . My head is spinning from people coming and going. It's been full on for me: swim party on the weekend, went to the Eagles (I didn't get home until three AM (*sssh*) and then went to a fiftieth birthday party next night. I took care of the group gift, but they exposed me as the buyer of the naughty boxers—pretty embarrassing!).

This week has been busy too—lots of meetings, my laptop crashed today (Charles's secretary, the sweetheart, met me and took it off to a repair shop, bless her heart), tomorrow night I'm out with the girls for a prerugby bash so it could be another scary late night (its Rugby Sevens weekend), Charles Jr. is having twenty-five people to dinner Friday night (assistant high school principal is coming too) . . . and I get to do it all myself. See, I can manage on my own if I have to. We'll see. I could have a breakdown by the weekend!

Heading to bed as Michael and I are up at 4:30 AM for his swimming practice. I'm *so* looking forward to summer and no routine!

Jx

Sent from my BlackBerry® wireless device

From: Abigail <Abigail@sympatico.ca>
Subject: Concert
Date: 23 March 2011, 2:26:33 PM EDT
To: Jenya <Jenya@hotmail.com>

Dear Jenya,

You impress me because you do manage a lot, but at the same time, you know how to have fun. I can imagine the Eagles concert was spectacular; "Desperado" is a favorite. Out at three AM—well done! Life is far too short not to live it fully. You made me laugh about the risky boxers. A party is as good as the laughter at it, so well done with the group gift!

Today is a complete snowstorm here. Deep, drifting, freezing, cold snow . . . school closures too. My daughter has baked white cupcakes, chocolate cupcakes, and made icing to put in the time.

I wish I could sit in on a Model UN conference. I would love to see how those meetings work—communication through interpreters, a great learning experience.

Twenty-five people for dinner? No problem. Set the table the night before, even if it is a buffet, get that all prettied up, then dial a caterer—the one with no guilt written beside their number. Then you won't be tired, unless you really want to cook for that many?

XOXO,
Abigail

From: Jenya <Jenya@hotmail.com>
Subject: Thai Food
Date: 12 April 2011, 7:26 AM
To: Abigail <Abigail@sympatico.ca>

Hi, Abigail,

Hope this e-mail finds you well.

Just returned from a few days in Bangkok with one of my best friends. We met when the kids were in preschool here and have remained good friends all these years despite her moving all over Europe and back to Asia again. She has a beautiful home there, so we relaxed by the pool. She took me to a great massage where they use herbal steam balls, did manicure and pedicures, yoga class, and even a Thai cooking class (a Japanese film crew was there, so I guess we will be on Japanese TV). Fun to get pampered for a few days and do girly things! Plus, I *love* Thai food. It's my favorite!

Back to reality this week.

Jx

PS, sounds like your plans for the UK are shaping up. What fun!

From: Abigail <Abigail@sympatico.ca>
Subject: Re: Thai Food
Date: 12 April 2011, 6:55:08 PM EDT
To: Jenya <Jenya@hotmail.com>

Dear Jenya,

Glad that you had sweet-pampering girl time in Bangkok. The herbal steam ball massage sounds like exotic Asian rejuvenation. And Thai food, always a tasty highlight. Sarah and I learned to cook pad Thai at a class here in the city. Newly married, I bravely took home the written instructions and made it for dinner guests. I explained to their meat-and-potato minds what it was, but they just looked at me blankly and asked for ketchup. So now when I find a Thai food-appreciating friend, I like to keep them.

Spring is struggling to stay its appearance. We've had dramatically interchangeable hot-and-cold weather all in one day for many days. On top of poor spring weather, I offered a minirant at book club last night because the science fiction novel one of the girls chose was nothing other than ghoulish rubbish, and I didn't even disguise my dislike of it. I did, however, pick *Sky Burial* as my selection for next month. I'm very excited to discuss it. But today, nothing helps the struggle to understand the many questions that seemingly have no forthcoming answers. I'm unable to type much on the topic. It's an over-tea kind of chat.

I'm off to step into my studio and mix oil colours for my next painting. It's a portrait of a child.

XO,
Abigail

From: Jenya <Jenya@hotmail.com>
Subject: London
Date: 29 June 2011, 10:03 AM
To: Abigail <Abigail@sympatico.ca>

Hi, Abigail,

Charles and I reviewed your e-mail and were talking about all the things we love to do in the UK. If you wish to splurge for your fortieth, Mandarin is very nice and so is the Cadogan Arms. We tend to stay in smaller places when we are there. The Lanesborough is a beautiful hotel (used to be an old hospital) where they serve a lovely afternoon tea. I haven't been for tea in a long time there, but Harrods and Fortnum & Mason were good places too. You have to see the Harrods food hall. We often pick up a few things and have a picnic in Hyde Park. Harvey Nichols's sushi bar is great and close to Mandarin. Evensong at Westminster Abbey is worth doing. As far as pubs go, there are so many to go to. They've changed a lot too as you can't smoke in them. So many have gone up market with nice dining rooms and good food. Very different from when we lived there! So many fabulous galleries to see too and great plays . . .

We have decided to come back to Canada early so we'll be up North for long weekend.

Hope to talk soon.

JX

From: Abigail <Abigail@sympatico.ca>
Subject: Re: London
Date: 29 June 2011, 10:06 PM
To: Jenya <Jenya@hotmail.com>

Jenya,

Thank you again and again for these London specifics. They are very
helpful.

Our guests from Alabama left this morning. If you are up and out on
the lake, do boat over.

On Wednesday I'm heading back to the city for three days. Hope your
week is going as perfectly as you planned it!

XO,
Abigail

From: Jenya <Jenya@hotmail.com>
Subject: This weekend
Date: 11 July 2011, 12:24 AM
To: Abigail <Abigail@sympatico.ca>

Hi, Abigail,

Finally got my blackberry working again!

Sorry to miss seeing you, but I'm still in London. Will be back at
the cottage hopefully this weekend, just waiting to hear Charles's
latest flight schedule. Has it rained up north this week as I'm so
worried about my hanging baskets, window boxes, and flowers on the
cottage patio?

Michael developed a shoulder injury last week, so we are icing it like crazy and have to see a massage therapist tomorrow. Thankfully, his coach here doesn't think it's his rotator cuff (muscle sprain, we hope), so fingers crossed, his swimming career is not over.

Having a good visit with my mom. We've been making jam and puttering away. Today she took me to a great Asian food market that just opened up. I thought I was back in Singapore! Couldn't get over all the great herbs and veggies. Guess who's making dinner next few nights here.

Charles Jr. e-mailed and said he successfully won a "Mandarin cooking utensil" contest when his class went to Chinatown, so he's excited to bring back a pair of "really long" chopsticks and a wok. Hilarious!

I'll call you when we are back up north.

Jx

From: Abigail <Abigail@sympatico.ca>
Subject: Re: This weekend
Date: 11 July 2011, 8:44:36 PM EDT
To: Jenya <Jenya@hotmail.com>

Dear Jenya,

Glad you are enjoying time with your mom—special days that can't be rushed. Did you make strawberry jam? It's the red berry season. Tess and I took a car full of children berry picking . . . then made jam, crisp, and pie! Sweet-strawberry, sunny-day happiness. The younger girls came up with a name; they called themselves the Sweetie Pies . . . took their jars of jam and baked goods in baskets for sale by boat around the bay. Saturday-morning-by-the-lake fun. I wanted the children to see, experience, and learn the process from start to finish—picking, making, selling. Not all adults hold this logic, so I persevered amidst opposition and tried to ensure the children did not get sidetracked in the three-day process. It drew the older girls and the younger ones together and might just be one highlight when we look back over the summer.

It hasn't rained although the forecast was calling for thunderstorms today. I can send one of the boys over to water your flowers if you'd like?

I'm so sorry to read about Michael. A career-altering injury. Oh no, bring on that ice. I have underlying fear of injury, knowing that it can derail very promising athletes. Coaches have insight and experience. Try to rest in the thought that this guy is right; it is just a bad sprain. Do they x-ray or ultrasound a shoulder?

Asian food market sounds fresh and enjoyable. I am having a foreign treat myself as my friend Madeline brought up takeout from our favorite Indian restaurant. That means I get to enjoy a glass of white wine and a taste of Bombay in Muskoka. I am halfway into Philippa Gregory's historical fiction about kings and queens. The Queen of France convinces her husband to grant her a divorce so she can marry an ambitious nineteen-year-old. In doing so, the two join regions, and not long after, they rule England. This author weaves a dramatic, romantic, and compelling tale. Do you have a reality-escaping summer read on the go?

It's Monday, and I am enjoying this first calm night visit typing at my leisure. There is no one at my harvest table for dinner for the first time in weeks. I'm not accustomed to the quiet. I will be very glad to welcome whoever is here and fill the kitchen up again—but after going to the Taylor Swift concert in the city. For now, it will be Joy and I meeting Tess and her daughter. The girls around the lake have made up dance routines to Taylor music. So cute.

Enjoy every step in London.

XO,
Abigail

From: Jenya <Jenya@hotmail.com>
Subject: Just Checking In
Date: 19 July 2011, 11:31 PM
To: Abigail <Abigail@sympatico.ca>

Hi, Abigail,

Just checking in to see how your week was.

Nice week with my mom, as always. Had a little outing with her to St. Mary's, visited relatives, and worked away in her garden. Her cucumbers are in, so we are enjoying those. My sister and I took her to lunch yesterday to celebrate her birthday early, so she enjoyed that. My other sister is at her cottage, so she missed out. I've been plowing through new project proposals this week. So good to get caught up on some of my foundation work. I think I've driven my poor nephew nuts making him print out all sorts of documents for me. Looking forward to dinner with my best friends tonight.

Charles Jr. called yesterday and is enjoying his trip with Dad. They sent me a photo of them enjoying clam chowder and lobster in Boston. I wrote back *jealous*.

My in-laws have changed their plans, so I won't be heading up tomorrow. I actually convinced them to head straight back up after Mom's appointment on Friday so they don't get caught in crazy traffic.

Don't really need that at their age. I'll now be picking up Charles and Charles Jr. from the airport on Saturday, so we'll be up after that.

See you soon,
Jx

From: Abigail <Abigail@sympatico.ca>
Subject: Lunch
Date: 20 July 2011, 11:23 AM
To: Jenya <Jenya@hotmail.com>

Jenya,

We had extended family staying here at the cottage for two days but now have a break before weekend guests. Let me know if lunch tomorrow works well for you.

XO

From: Jenya <Jenya@hotmail.com>
Subject: Re: Lunch
Date: 21 July 2011, 2:18 AM
To: Abigail <Abigail@sympatico.ca>

Hi, Abi,

Tried to call you this morning but no answer. Shall I pick you up at 11:30 AM?

Just dropping Michael at camp here, so sorry if I'm curt.

Jx

From: Abigail <Abigail@sympatico.ca>
Subject: Perfect
Date: 21 July 2011, 5:21:41 PM EDT
To: Jenya <Jenya@hotmail.com>

11:30 AM is perfect. Will try to tame cottage hair for the occasion. :-)

From: Abigail <Abigail@sympatico.ca>
Subject: Settled Home
Date: 30 August 2011, 12:58:02 AM EDT
To: Jenya <Jenya@hotmail.com>

Dear Jenya,

Glad to hear that you have begun the Singapore fall schedule run well! It is just a sweet welcome routine when things get back on track . . . children settled at school, a tougher professional coach welcomed, board meeting scheduled, and a trip in store for next week. Well done! That all takes effort.

It was Elizabeth Gilbert that told me of the intense poverty in Cambodia. Vietnam must be very similar. I have a soft spot for gentle Vietnamese people, imagining some as stowaways in the hull of a ship—although there has to be so much more to their beautiful culture than the escape of it. You will have a very worthwhile trip and feel the accomplishment of reaching your fall foundation work goals. It is amazing to have a plan, to see it take shape, and to help other's by the effort of it. Take pictures while you are there, and please tell me all about it . . . so I can see and learn.

I am typing to you from my desk in the city, after an excellent last week at the cottage with my father. Joy and William were with us as George went back to the city early for training camp. My dad is in surprisingly steady health. He has a gentle, understanding nature and is a very supportive presence. We thoroughly relaxed and enjoyed the visit together. I had older guests over for tea and others for dinner, people my dad knew well and was glad to reconnect with. We also hunkered down during the tornado warning and, despite that somewhat stressful stormy evening, agreed that the girls could invite people for a year-end bonfire. My father's visit concluded this cottaging season on a splendid note!

Jenya, as I packed my luggage to leave, I made a mental note of that old phrase "less is more." I took it to heart not only about the clothes that I didn't wear. So as to pack less next summer, only bring the favorites; the rest won't get worn anyway. And the thought that less of my own agenda meant more for my daughter . . . as I knelt in the cupboard and folded, it all made sense to me. Less is more. The four books that I could easily read in a summer, this year was one. The series of paintings that I had in mind to complete was just a flimsy underpainting. The travel scrapbook that I intended to assemble . . . yes, just a stack of unassembled photographs. But, Jenya, my daughter had a full, happy, solid summer—the best that I could make it for her. And since she'll be turning fifteen next summer or the following one, she'll likely be getting a job. This sunny-season window is equally as precious as it is short . . . fold, pack, fold, pack . . .

I'll read more books the summer that she is off working, but for this summer, the book basket was carted home with sweet memories of teenage girls giggling while baking, of making colourful string bracelets, of jumping off the rock together at Blueberry Island, of her smiling, suntanned face framed with caramel-coloured curls. It is simple: "less is more." This summer, less for me meant much more for my teenage daughter and her friends. Which actually was a perfect summer, one that ended with my dad on a splendid orange sunset note.

Now I can't tell you that the adjustment to the city is lovely. I do miss the Muskoka Lake fresh air, cannot stand the sight of large spaces of concrete, and confess am not yet actually organized for fall. Once Staples has satisfied our school supply needs, new running shoes are neatly ready in a row, school uniforms are tried on to fit . . . well, that's it. City life hits. I think it's because one browse at the latest fall fashions for me is enough. Chatting with hockey parents at the team social was an attempt to infuse sincere enthusiasm into a thick, tired parent atmosphere. Plus my own class schedule has yet to be written in. Starbucks helps. As soon as I get my painting classes organized and fit in yoga or Pilates, I'll be ready to rock. Well, rock the fall, providing I ignore what I clearly don't want to admit to myself and that I stack up all the positives. Like the two fortieth birthday parties that I get to go to before mine and, yes, my make-it-to-England trip! Even at the risk of fully boring you, I am still going to tell you everything that I get to see and do because I will be so thrilled, and you will know what I mean.

Sarah—bless her detailed, well-organized heart—has an agenda typed up for us. Little by little we are filling in the days, choosing events and activities. We arrive on September 26, early morning, rent a car, and head to Oxford then to Stratford through the Cotswolds. We plan to drive up to Ettington and, from there, make our way back down through towns called Upper and Lower Slaughter, Stow-on-the-Wold, and possibly to Bath before taking in Windsor Castle and then on into London. We've booked a show at the Globe and planned to go to Evensong at Westminster. That's a sketch, but the details are taking fine, hand-painted, bone china shape. :-)

Must sign off now because it's late and I've chatted on and on. A habit of mine to blather and describe everything while talking with my hands. Husband hates it and is trying to train me to not use my arms when I talk. I'm self-conscious about it now but really rather use my hands to get the overflowing chatter across. I am sure no one can understand me unless I wave my arms around. It doesn't make half as much sense, don't you think? Ha ha ha.

Must run. Big hugs and safety as you travel to Cambodia.

XOXO,
Abigail

From: Jenya <Jenya@hotmail.com>
Subject: Less is More
Date: 31 August 2011, 8:37 AM
To: Abigail <Abigail@sympatico.ca>

Hi, Abigail,

"Less is more." Love that! On my charity trips, this is so true. The people I visit have so little, but they have so much more than we do in terms of the support in their communities. I've attached a piece I wrote from one of my first trips to Sichuan to work with the leprosy sufferers. Hope you enjoy it.

I honestly think you should try to write for a paper or see if a magazine would pick up a piece on "The Last Days Of Summer." You have a talent and an ability to describe the time with your dad and the experience it was for your daughter so eloquently. I have some ideas for children's books but don't think I could write as beautifully as you in my average e-mail.

I'm so excited about your trip to London, and no, you won't bore me with any of the details. I *love* London, apart from the weather. I was very sad to leave it! But Asia has offered so much excitement and adventure to my life. Although there are many things I miss about Canada, I love the energy here! Cambodia and Vietnam are incredible places. I don't have as much time there as I would like but am excited to make a change for many street kids in Cambodia and disabled kids in Vietnam! I am visiting two new destinations in both countries I've never been to before, so I'm quite excited and looking forward to a new challenge!

The new swim coach is very capable, and our first board meeting of the season went well today (three hours, mind you). I pulled my hair out all afternoon as my social events are not coming together with the new training schedule. We do not have all groups training on the same days as before, which makes it difficult to get everyone together at the same time. I spent my afternoon looking through school calendars, SAT dates, after-school activities, and major events and put together a proposal. Let's hope it works!

Charles and I are in negotiations at the moment for a new family office and living quarters for us. Don't want to jinx it, but if all comes through, we'll be busy doing designs and renovating all that in the coming months. Managed to extend our lease here until June so as not to disrupt the boys. Busy doing school applications for both Charles Jr. and Michael on top of that. Deep breathing and take it one day at a time.

Meeting up with Sarah on Monday for a coffee, so look forward to hearing more about your trip. *Lucky.* Wish I could join you!

Good luck with the start of school.

Jx

PS, You must be part European with that hand waving/gesturing. A good thing! Shows emotion and zest for life!

From: Abigail <Abigail@sympatico.ca>
Subject: Stilettos
Date: 31 August 2011, 11:08:38 PM EDT
To: Jenya <Jenya@hotmail.com>

Jenya,

I can hear your heart for the Yi people, can envision the mountain villages, and can understand their hurt at being put out from their families. Of all the many causes to support, this has to be the best one because these people are the most marginalized. They are like the untouchables in India, a silent group of sufferers. I can imagine the first few people taking refuge in the mountains years ago. The one or two must have carved out a means of survival, word would have spread, and other hurt, lame, and shunned souls would slowly make their way one by one up the mountain trail, hoping for refuge. Eventually, whole communities would have formed. Do you know how many years the villages have existed? It is heart wrenching and hopeful at the very same time! I so enjoyed reading about your work—loved it. Jenya, you do write very well; don't set aside the idea to write a children's book. In fact, put it on your list of to-dos if you can for this fall.

It's funny about writing: when I try to write seriously, it can be a chore. However, when I trust someone enough, I type-talk to them. Just my thoughts spilling out, trusting that my friend gets me. Always, by then I know the person well enough to be pretty sure that they will understand my spilling, so talking is natural—no struggle at all. Waving hands and all. In order to write an article or a book for that matter, I'd have to get over the fear that my tumbling thoughts would not be understood. I'll consider what you suggested and try.

Well done compiling schedules and finding time to fit in swim team social events. Don't lose sight of how important the social aspect is. It is high priority . . . social events draw the team together, infuse all the fun, facilitate deeper relationships, and are huge for morale. Keep at it because this year might just be the best one you've organized so far.

Also, enjoy looking for and planning on moving. A move is always exciting. It allows for a fresh, new start in many ways—fresh paint, exciting decorating palette, and personally created happy atmosphere. Enjoy the rush of all of that!

Hug Sarah for me. Tell her I'm bringing stilettos—just kidding, walking shoes. Well, maybe one pair of splendid shoes—Just in case we go out on London town and don't have to walk far. :-) Yes! Prada: brown leather. They screamed *England* and I listened.
:-)
XO,
Abigail

From: Abigail <Abigail@sympatico.ca>
Subject: Castle Combe
Date: 5 October 2011, 16:50:47
To: Jenya <Jenya@hotmail.com>

Jenya,

It's as if the gods dropped mounds of green velvet and then scattered it with spots of white wool. I have never seen such an expanse of graceful, rolling hills decorated with so many grazing sheep. The most fun was navigating, with map in hand, to each little town along the way. This picture was taken having high tea in Castle Combe, one of the prettiest villages in all of England. And the pubs have sofas!

They do. Armchairs and sofas by crackling fireplaces, where they serve the tastiest pub fare—warm comfort and welcomingly delicious. The Ritz was old-world-city style with earpiece-wearing security doormen, who seriously guarded our every move. They broke composure and cracked a smile on our third-day stay! The castles, the palace, Oxford, and Evensong . . . I'm seriously in love with this country. There is a serene order, an academic atmosphere, and an old-world, steadfast feel. They value fine china, lace, and tea at its cream-with-honey best. I hope you are relaxing, sipping tea or sake, whichever the day calls for. :-)

Jet-lagged love from Canada,
Abigail

From: Jenya <Jenya@hotmail.com>
Subject: Fabulous
Date: 6 October 2011, 12:04 AM
To: Abigail <Abigail@sympatico.ca>

Hi, Abi,

I am so happy you had such a fabulous trip! "Brill," as the Brits say!
England is wonderful and brings back such great memories of living
there. There is so much to see and do in London, and yet it is so easy
to escape to the beautiful countryside that you described. That is one
thing I really miss about living in Singapore . . . hard to get into a car
and drive to the country, and as exotic as many of the places are in
Asia, you never find pretty villages like you do in Europe. They are
magical! Charles and I often escaped to the coast or would get away
for the weekend and go riding in the Cotswolds when we lived there.
In London, one of my favorite things to do was to get up early on a
Sunday and hit the Shoreditch market, grab the *Sunday Times*, and
read it over salmon and lox bagels. The pubs have changed so much,
gone from smoke dens to warm, cozy places with fine dining! The
Brits are indeed very civilized. They seem to bring order wherever
they go. In Asia, they were instrumental in setting up the great
infrastructure and efficient public transportation system, insisted on
good court systems, eradicated corruption, and of course, introduced
their lovely linens and high tea here! Don't know if you've read Bill
Bryson's book called *Notes from a Small Island* . . . a must-read now
that you have been there. Recently read *Cutting for Stone* too, which
was a brilliant book!

We had a public holiday here yesterday. Charles was working in the
office, catching up as he'd been away for several weeks. And boys
were doing homework, so I took a long walk by myself through the
country park. The trail winds its way from one end of the south side
to the other . . . beautiful views of the ocean, lush green mountains,
and no sounds but the chirping of birds. So many people never see this
side of the area when they visit. I came home feeling refreshed.

Are you heading to the cottage for Thanksgiving? We are having some friends here to dinner Saturday night.

Jx

PS, I heard you had a great birthday bash! Lots of fun and great speeches!

From: Abigail <Abigail@sympatico.ca>
Subject: Re: Fabulous
Date: 6 October 2011, 10:29:28 PM EDT
To: Jenya <Jenya@hotmail.com>

Jenya,

Thank you for being happy for me and for sharing appreciation for both British countryside and culture. Not everyone has the same taste. Even my pictures bored my husband, so I did as he asked and fast-forwarded them to the end. Old stone buildings are not for everyone . . . that's understandable.

I did read Bryson's book; I'd been given it about a year ago. Maybe I should reread it to refresh my memory now that I can envision details of the countryside better? Your long walk through the park sounds invigorating. I love exercise like that; it feels amazing. Each fall, I try to get out in the morning to run the hill down to the river behind my house. It's not a long run, but it is a great way to begin the day because the fresh fall air is healthy, and the early morning river looks so pretty. I won't run tomorrow morning; have to drive Joy to early morning basketball practice at her high school and then on to Friday's painting class. Will not go to the cottage this weekend; both boys have hockey. Will set the dining room table and make dinner here in the city. I love Thanksgiving . . . the smell of turkey dinner roasting, hopefully some shepherds pie with lamb, and maybe a homemade pie . . . if I'm energetic . . . and always, always so much to be thankful for.

Yes, had a fantastic time at my party! I am still very grateful for all who were able to celebrate with me. Friends' speeches were kind and funny. Three of my closest girls, each without knowing the others' dress selection for the evening, wore bright red dresses . . . very dazzling blondes in bright red. They looked stunning! It was *so* great. Just loved the night of dining and dancing.

I'm unwaveringly happy to be older and deeply appreciate life. A certain confidence comes with quiet assurance. I think criticism is easier to take because you just know who you are and why you choose to do what you do.

Fully enjoy dinner with friends. Thanks again for being interested in England.

XOXO,
Abigail

From: Jenya <Jenya@hotmail.com>
Subject: Happy New Year
Date: 1 January 2012, 3:59 PM
To: Abigail <Abigail@sympatico.ca>

Hi, Abigail,

Happy New Year! Hope you had a lovely celebration and a good start to 2012.

Sorry it has taken me this long to reply to your e-mail. It was a crazy few days when we arrived in Canada, and then we were off to Florida. The weather was perfect, and we ended up buying a boat. So lots to coordinate on that end, but we enjoyed it immensely. Charles and Charles Jr. had some great father-son fishing trips and managed to get some good catches. Michael also invited some swimming buddies onboard one day. We had our long bike rides and long beach walks, so it was a very relaxing time.

I'm at my mom's now. So good to have time with her, but this weather is atrocious! I took a long walk this afternoon but glad I have a guest pass to my sister's gym starting tomorrow . . . will be my retreat if this weather keeps up. I actually have a busy week. My sister and I are off to the movies tomorrow, seeing my best friends on Tuesday, then getting together with Charles's sister, my old politics professor, and other friends. Also have to throw Russian Christmas in there and back on a plane to Singapore Saturday night.

My computer also crashed a few days ago, so have to get a new one. Thankfully, my fourteen-year-old nephew is an IT genius and managed to take out hard disc and copy my docs onto a CD. He also said he'd help me with new setup, so should be good to go again soon. Maybe a new computer for the New Year is a sign of luck?

Sarah's news is exciting . . . will be sad to lose her to Malaysia, but will be a great adventure. I'm ready for a new one myself! Burma is calling . . .

Looking forward to hearing all your holiday news.

Jx

Sent from my BlackBerry® wireless device

From: Abigail <Abigail@sympatico.ca>
Subject: Re: Happy New Year!
Date: 3 January 2012, 5:39:05 PM EST
To: Jenya <Jenya@hotmail.com>

Jenya,

Happy 2012 to you too! I love the fresh white squares on the new paper calendar. Days ready to be penciled in with plans and

possibilities . . . for me each weekend in January is organized, my
art school schedule very happily registered for. Today I got into the
classes that come highly recommended. But first, I'm very glad that
you have had very sunny boating, beach-walking holidays. Florida
sounds amazing. Amidst international travel, you deserve those lovely
days, precious time with your boys, and exciting fun cruising the ocean
on a new boat! So nice too that you have days with your mom and
sister, highlight conversations, and that holy ornate Russian Christmas
celebration you've described to me before must just be the crown on
Christmas! Enjoy these Canadian-taken steps. Your friends will be so
glad to see you, to catch up, and to look forward to the New Year
together in friendship, even if countries apart.

I did my best to make Christmas lovely . . . Christmas Eve, many
mini candlelights brought a warm glow and peace that I'd envisioned.
I did take a number of leisurely evenings and even some oddly green
grass holiday afternoons sipping tea by crackling fire and drinking in
holiday calm by myself—if you don't count my new kitten who purrs
and is soft, furry company. That guilt-free calm was after my in-law
family of thirty people celebrated for five flowing, festive days . . .
cousins' sleepover, meals hosted and attended from house to restaurant
to house again; it flowed. At one point, my daughter and her three
girl cousins were sleeping over at their grandma's; my husband was
at the tournament hockey game with one son; my brother-in-law was
in the guest room bed, ill and dizzy with stress; my nephew slid his
jeep into the snowy night ditch at the bottom of our laneway; and I'd
lost track of how many of the nineteen grandchildren were playing
ping-pong in my basement. I didn't know what to do first: run upstairs
with a cold cloth or outside with a shovel. Amidst it all, I met my
brother-in-law's new girlfriend while dearly missing his wife, showed
a DVD of my in-law's Christmas ten years ago, and watched as the
children marveled at themselves so long ago. And I seemed to make
meals continually. So with turkey stew all simmered and saved frozen,
only shortbread crumbs left in the container, the decorations spotlessly
cleaned up and put away—January needed to be welcomed, which led
to the sweetest three days of the whole holidays spent, just my daughter

and I. The boys had gone to the cottage to glance disappointedly at the closed skiddoo trails while she and I stayed in the city. We, Christmas knitted-hat wearing, sauntered along lakeshore, chatted with the butcher, the baker, and the fish market fellow . . . purchased treats for our small but specially planned New Year's Eve dinner. Made even-bright strawberries dipped in milk chocolate to welcome the fresh white squares on the paper calendar! A sweet three days. So my squares of penciled-in, to-look-forward-to plans include Deerhurst Resort with my daughter next weekend and New York City on the twenty-fourth to twenty-ninth.

Must go. Finishing a painting that I've been working on for my sister, wanting to send it before meeting her in NYC.

Holiday hugs and huge happiness for your January white-square plans and possibilities.

XOXOXO,
Abigail

From: Abigail <Abigail@sympatico.ca>
Subject: Reading
Date: 19 January 2012, 2:17 AM
To: Jenya <Jenya@hotmail.com>

Jenya,

We are eighteen days into the New Year. Can you believe it? I'm searching for a friend who has read the book entitled *Atlas Shrugged* by Ayn Rand. Lisa recommended it. An American classic? I'd never heard of it before. I'm only 342 pages into its 1,168-page-thick read . . . very multilayered, fascinating, compelling discussion—demanding. Any chance you've read it? Also, I previously finished *I Shall Not Hate* by Dr. Izzeldin Abuelaish, set in the Gaza Strip, a Palestinian physician who works in a hospital in Israeli loses his daughters in the bombing of January 2009. It's an easy, heart-wrenching, amidst-war-in-Gaza read, one to add to your list.

XOXO,
Abigail

From: Jenya <Jenya@hotmail.com>
Subject: Re: Reading
Date: 18 January 2012, 9:09 PM
To: Abigail <Abigail@sympatico.ca>

Hi, Abigail,

Nice to hear from you. Been a hectic start to the year. Only been back two weeks and off to Sri Lanka tomorrow. Ayn Rand on my bookshelf, but haven't read. It's one of my friend's favorite books. The Palestinian one sounds very interesting. Haven't read much since I've been back, except newspapers and magazines. Feb to June is going to be crazy with office move, home move, swim stuff, sorting boys to leave . . . deep breaths, lots of lists, and taking it one day at a time . . .

Had a big going-away party for Michael's swim buddy last night. It was supposed to be at someone else's house, and then Michael announced the change at the last minute! I stayed calm and thought, *I'll be missing this next year!* Doing my lai see packets at the moment . . . tradition to hand out money to guards, hairdressers, friends' children, favorite waiters, etc., after Chinese New Year.

Just finished my New Year foundation newsletter . . . lots going on there too. Should send you a copy so you can see what we're up to.

Have to run. Hope all is well with you.

Hugs,
Jx

From: Abigail <Abigail@sympatico.ca>
Subject: Re: Reading
Date: 19 January 2012, 2:38:19 PM EST
To: Jenya <Jenya@hotmail.com>

Hi, Jenya,

Yes, please send me your newsletter. I would love to read the update! It would be fun to make up packets to celebrate the Chinese New Year. Do you know, for the first time that I remember, the local Walmart had an entire row of bright red Chinese New Year decorations on display for sale. They might well be the American version of the real thing, kind of like what chicken balls are to the food court. But nevertheless, it was interesting to see even a mainstream American box store acknowledge Chinese culture.

You've heard of Ayn Rand! Well, if you see a window of time to read it—even in the next year or two—remember me because I need a discussion partner or two to fully comprehend all the layers. I am loving it so far. If your friend would consider sharing highlight insights, give them my e-mail. Maybe I can get an online discussion going . . . it's that kind of a book. You must be so looking forward to all the changes. Can you have everything freshly decorated and most things set up before you move from where you are living now? It all takes a lot of organization, preparation, and planning. I typed to Sarah the other day and said that most women just couldn't do what is required of you girls to do in order to move a family and live in a foreign country. It takes much competence, planning, and detailed organization. Well done, girls, for making it all happen, for making a move flow with ease and detailed order . . . all appearing effortless. These men have outstanding wives who competently cover much!

Must run. Joy has four friends over for lunch, celebrating their last day of exams—so sweet to see them relieved after much studying. All is well.

XO,
Abi

From: Abigail <Abigail@sympatico.ca>
Subject: Travel
Date: 1 February 2012, 10:19:09 AM EST
To: Jenya <Jenya@hotmail.com>

Jenya,

How was Sri Lanka? Hope you are fully enjoying the trip, seeing your ideas accomplished, or settled back in after it all. There is always detailed planning that goes into travel . . . a serious satisfaction when you see it all take a no-hitch, quick-flight, dinner-reservation-appointment-meeting shape. Then this momentary adjustment after travel, the need to refocus and plan ahead. I'm stuck in the momentary adjustment mode today . . . can't believe it is already the beginning of February. New York was its wonderful-hotel, favorite-Luxembourg-restaurant-night light self . . . .

Thinking of you, hoping you are having a calm-sipping-tea day.

XO,
Abigail

From: Jenya <Jenya@hotmail.com>
Subject: Re: Travel
Date: 1 February 2012, 8:11 PM
To: Abigail <Abigail@sympatico.ca>

Dear Abigail,

Very nice to hear from you. Did you go to New York with friends?

Below are some photos from our safari in Sri Lanka. We met friends from the UK while we're there. Older couple . . . he does all the makeup for the Hollywood actors . . . so interesting fellow.

Our trip was fantastic. We started off in the north where we saw elephants bathing at an orphanage, hiked, and toured the tea plantations. We then headed to the south where we went on safari . . . so nice to sleep in tents, enjoy the stars at night (and a few crocodile sightings in the marsh nearby), and race around by day, trying to find "the creatures." We went to see the children at the school that we sponsored after the safari, took the boys to see Galle (an old Dutch fort, which is now a World Heritage site), and then relaxed on the beach at our favorite place for two days, Bentota.

I have been thinking a lot about what you had to say about the boys in your last e-mail. They are lucky to have been exposed to so much travel and cultures, but I also think they have given up many things as expat kids . . . having a paper route, being near family and close friends, getting their driver's license at sixteen . . . well, not long before they head off to the real world with boarding school and university. Best of both worlds, I guess. Guess it will be the same for me next year as I run between both places.

Hope you are well.

Jx

From: Abigail <Abigail@sympatico.ca>
Subject: Experiences
Date: 2 February 2012, 5:06:17 PM EST
To: Jenya <Jenya@hotmail.com>

Jenya,

The photographs are spectacular; what lovely sights! Sleeping in tents with animals all roaming freely in the wild right next to you! So great to see these shots. Can feel the humidity and hear the sounds of the rainforest. The elephants are especially magnificent. Did you read the novel *Water for Elephants*? Photos made me remember Rosie, the smart elephant who understood Polish but was severely punished for not obeying her cruel trainer's commands in English. Amazing, isn't it that there is such contrast in beauty, from the delicate, flighty, brilliantly feathered bird to the massive, solid, lumbering elephant? So much to see, admire, and learn about. The sweet, wide-eyed children at the school must have been a huge highlight—big smiles with changed lives. That's what those little ones have.

New York was preplanned with my father and sister. Pamela and I had taken our daughters to the city when they were ten. Now, five years later, the two girls both fifteen years old, experienced the city at a whole new level.

Just Joy and I flew to Rhode Island and spent three days at my father's house. I took her to the Vanderbilt's Breakers, toured Salve Regina because it is so close, saw U of RI campus, and talked about Brown. Dad and his wife, Joy, and I took the train together into Penn Station just for the experience and then spent three days in NYC. A show, my favorite restaurants, strolling SoHo . . . . My sister, the two girls, and I stayed up until three AM the night she flew in. Just couldn't stop the glass-of-wine-laughing fun! I'm still very grateful that it worked out. Saved air miles, planned details, argued for clearance ahead . . . . Do you think that one day my daughter will understand how much I fought for—for her? Children may only know their parents' sacrifice one day if they are called to make the same. But my fifteen-year-old, happily hailing her first yellow cab, will never know that had I given up, we wouldn't have made it there.

It is the same for you, Jenya. Your boys might never fully know how much you missed your family or the details you personally have adjusted to be living in Asia. But they have had fascinating, adventurous, educational lives and are, for sure, better men for it.

I think it may feel somewhat stunning when your boys move ahead, even though it is naturally the right time. They are well prepared, very capable . . . . I think the lurch in a mother's heart is momentous. Have you asked other mothers who have helped their children move out and settle how they found the adjustment? I've heard that the relationship changes to a new adult level, that calls home are just to talk, which feels very good. I feel that so much energy is spent right now, making the lives of these children flow well . . . meals, transportation, homework help, and more meals. In which the French cast iron pot simmers a mighty fine stew on a February day. But the fullness of life is the overflowing upholding of the children, with the aside things of oneself fit into the spaces in between—like my nice art teacher class tomorrow! So yes—when I imagine children moved ahead, I can see an entirely new picture. And your new picture will be this September . . . huuumn . . . that calls for longer talks and courage in who you are and where you want to go. If I had that exactly down, perfectly pat myself, I'd fax it to you. But I'm needing all the courage I can count.

Hey, have typed out my favorite quotes from Ayn Rand. I haven't found a single person who's read it, other than Lisa, who kindly recommended it. How could I have overlooked such brilliance on my previous heard-about, need-to-read list? But must go now. The simple task of putting away groceries awaits.

XOXO,
Abigail

From: Jenya <Jenya@hotmail.com>
Subject: The Lady
Date: 6 February 2012, 06:55:21
To: Abigail <Abigail@sympatico.ca>

Info on the movie *The Lady: Aung San Suu Kyi.*

http://www.mizzima.com/edop/features/5868-plotting-the-lady-movie.html

Hi, Abi,

Just found and forwarded this link to a friend. Trying to convince her to see the movie with me this weekend as Christopher will be out of town. Thought you'd enjoy the synopsis. Have you seen it?

Sadly, I have not read *Water for Elephants*. Definitely on my list, as are so many other books. After being back in Sri Lanka, I really want to find a good read on the tea plantation area. Would love to hear more about the Brits' adventures, creating "Little England" and taking over the whole tea industry. Although I've been to Sri Lanka a few times, I learned on this trip that the island was a coffee producer. When the crops were damaged by disease, they switched to tea, and that is when the Brits moved in . . . of course, other political reasons after the Dutch were there.

I'm so glad you had a great time in New York with your sister and girls. It is so nice to have a getaway and good bonding time with Joy. Being in a household of men, I sometimes wish I had a daughter I could do girly things with. I can pretend when I'm on the ground doing my charity work! Michael just celebrated his sixteenth birthday with a group of boys. We went for Peking duck (his favorite), and the boys provided good entertainment. Lots of fun and good conversation . . . quite surprising for a table of teenagers! I have to say, our time in Sri Lanka was good bonding time as a family, especially on safari. There was no Wi-Fi, so we had lots of time to discuss ideas under the stars with other guests. And the boys did a lot of talking in their tent (good to have no devices!).

Life is hectic here and so many changes . . . new office is near completion. We decided to find a different flat rather than try to combine both, so I am flying around like mad, trying to find a new home. Think I have found two I like, fingers crossed. Waiting for boys' acceptances, getting them ready for their service trips to Laos and Chiang Mai, lots of socials coming up for the swim team. Our two new foundation projects from last year are off the ground and are now in the process of signing on two new projects. One is in Cambodia, and other one is helping Burmese students with their university education. I am also looking at a few things in Singapore. Once our website is updated, I'll send you the link. I was asked to speak at a foundation conference in Spain in March but turned it down (actually, public speaking is my worst nightmare, but I have been known to do it). Too much going on this year and feel I'll have more to share next year.

Don't know if I told you but my best friend is getting married after being single all these years. She focused on her career for many years and has met a lovely guy . . . . She is moving to Florida next month. They'll have a civil wedding there, and then she has her church wedding in Canada in October. The fall is going to be busy for me, with getting the boys sorted. I'll be doing some renovations at the cottage. Plan to have a shower at our place in Florida with the girls and then the big wedding to attend. So you might be seeing more of me . . . .

Time to pick up Charles from school, and then I need to go to the gym. Been working away at my computer all afternoon and am ready for a run!

Take care,
Jx

From: Abigail <Abigail@sympatico.ca>
Subject: Re: The Lady
Date: 10 February 2012, 2:40:34 PM EST
To: Jenya <Jenya@hotmail.com>

Hi, Jenya,

Thanks for typing. I am very glad to have a moment of quiet at my desk to write back. Today began with an early morning whirl of activity that immediately calmed when the front door closed. I helped two prepare and get out to school for the day while getting two others packed as they caught a flight to Quebec City this morning. It will be a five-day hockey tournament—possibly longer, depending on how the team does. After focused commotion to help it all take shape, I waved good-bye, closed the door, and calm instantly flooded. You know, the good feeling when all that you can do for your family is done and everyone is happily out and on their way. So it is Joy, William, and I here for the next while. William has an away game, so I'll be heading there on Sunday.

I loved reading the movie link and have seen a trailer or two about the movie. It looks amazing. I read that Feb 3 was the gala premiere in Singapore. It opens on April 27, 2012, in Canadian theaters, the press in Asia carrying it. But so far, little mention here, so really appreciated the link. Would love to hear if you saw the movie and how it was!

And yes, please do send your website. Would love to read up about your projects. The leprosy villages? The most wonderful thing is when something begins small, sustains itself, and grows. Sometimes I have a reminder of the power of perseverance even in my own tiny world . . . .

OK, I must stop chatting and go. But exciting that your best friend is getting married. That is lovely. You can look forward to celebrating with her. Maybe we could plan to have dinner or meet for lunch in Oakville one day after the October wedding. Hopefully, some summertime visits too, but if you are in Canada longer, book me in. I'd drag you to an art gallery or even to Langdon Hall for fall tea.

Hope you are feeling encouraged as you run, that the choice of living space is easy to find and perfectly suited to what you want, and that you just have an excellent day.

XO,
Abigail

From: Jenya <Jenya@hotmail.com>
Subject: Our Good News
Date: 15 February 2012, 4:17 AM
To: Abigail <Abigail@sympatico.ca>

Hi, Abi,

We got a very nice Valentine's Day treat. We learned Charles got accepted into University in Connecticut, so he is overjoyed. We are so proud of him. It's a wonderful liberal arts school, small classes. But what I really love is they take 47 percent of their students on financial aid. Not many schools are that generous and will provide for a great mix of kids. It's been a long journey, and now some of the pressure is off . . . waiting for final acceptance for Michael to come through on Mar 1.

We went to see *The Lady*. Although the reviews here were not great, have to say June and I really enjoyed it. A little too much violence for our liking, but was a compelling story, showed how supportive her family was and what she had to give up to try to achieve democracy in Burma.

Most of our website is now updated, if you want to have a look. I put together the website a few years ago with the help of a design team. Most of the photos are children from my leprosy project. One of my friends helped me make the photos look "older," like the *Life* photos. Trying to keep it as current as possible. Two more new projects coming online soon.

Had a fun fondue evening with Sarah and another friend last Saturday. Great to catch up. Guess she's off to KL this weekend . . . good timing as weather is not great here!

Hope all is well.

Jx

From: Abigail <Abigail@sympatico.ca>
Subject: Re: Our Good News
Date: 15 February 2012, 12:30:15 PM EST
To: Jenya <Jenya@hotmail.com>

Jenya,

Very touching to see your pictures, to read about the foundation, and to feel insight into each country. When you mention having a full plate, my goodness, this is why . . . a full plate in such a good way . . . upholding and overseeing each project, making decisions on what needs to meet when, structuring each initiative to sustain itself, propelling each one forward . . . . Plus choosing new ones! Seeing smiles on the faces of the children leaning over schoolbooks made possible by someone who cares enough to give for their education. Oh, Jenya, brings tears actually. Made me think of the quote "There can be no keener revelation of a societies soul than the way it treats its children." You must just love your work. The reward of visiting a site would be like an emotional river overflowing.

Great news for Charles—he will have excellent years there. Yes, a small student body by comparison but spectacular campus with private, secure feeling. I know academics are the main focus for these years, but when considering safety and security, social dimension, athletics, and study abroad opportunities—with all of that in mind—I think the smaller universities offer a superior all-round experience. Well, that's said after only touring one, Salve, and clearly not having a child at that stage yet. Big decision made, acceptance celebrating—a lot to look forward to! Well done, Charles.

George is on the ice as I type. They beat Switzerland yesterday and are hoping for a win today. International hockey teams are offering tough competition, so we'll see! High pressure and excitement for a twelve-year-old.

You saw the movie! She didn't get to raise her sons or see her dying husband one day. Will her personal choice be the stepping stone to freedom in her country? Will her sacrifice be worth it? I want to read about her husband, what kind of man would understand the big picture to that extent. An academic . . . . What did he teach? I must Google him and read up.

Have to go. I get so easily lost in type-chatting, and time gets away on me. Can you tell?

XOXO,
Abi

From: Abigail <Abigail@sympatico.ca>
Subject: Omani Princess
Date: 27 February 2012, 3:15:36 PM EST
To: Jenya <Jenya@hotmail.com>

Jenya,

Hope your day is highlighted with happiness, even if that means a glass of sparkling white over lunch, a list of to-dos well checked off, or a good book mid read. Any chance you've been following Syria? The most recent is the loss of Britain's *Sunday Times* foreign correspondent Marie Colvin and the photographer R. Ochlik. Reading the paper sure puts my simmering spaghetti sauce in perspective and stops me midday . . . . Today's *Globe* has a stunning picture of Aung San Suu Kyi waving from a vehicle in a foggy sunset. The caption says she is arriving to deliver an election speech at a rally in a village just outside Myanmar. It's their bravery that is so inspiring. During these February evenings, I need the newspaper to burn under the kindling in the fireplace. I find myself not burning the newspaper; instead, I'm saving articles. I know the news is all online, but I'm old-fashioned. I can't even bring myself to get an electronic book. I have to hold the real thing. Joy showed me a picture of the coolest loft library, with books up to and filling an entire wall right up to the peaked-roof ceiling. I saw the picture on Instagram, the iPhone app where people post excellent photographs. I only have it because I have a fifteen-year-old who smartly enough is doing exactly what I did at that age. Promising to share the new American Eagle sweater that we buy because then it's really only half price. Oh my, there are lovely, happy details to laugh at in a day, aren't there? For me, it's shared sweaters and baked cupcakes . . . kitchen all floured up freshly made.

Oh, Jenya, Aung San Suu Kyi speaking openly in public places for this campaign with no glass shield, just out in the open . . . . She'll be OK, won't she? Remember Benazir Bhutto? She was only fifty-four. They took her in 2007. I'm stirring sauce and fearing for these women . . . .

Must go, but here's thinking of Asma and her criticized high heels. If she's got to walk fearfully close to dictators, well by God she might as well wear vogue sunglasses and fantastic pumps. Jenya, her mother could very well have named her after David Austin's antique English rose, Sharifa Asma. A little girl named after a light pink rose is, in my mind, nothing other than intelligent, kind, and refined. When I look below the water, Omani princess Rose has no way of escape.

Remember, sparkling white over lunch. Wish I could sip a glass with you.

XOXO,
Abi

From: Jenya <Jenya@hotmail.com>
Subject: Ring
Date: 4 March 2012
To: Abigail <Abigail@symapatico.ca>

Abigail,

Do you have time for a phone call? I can ring you if you let me know when.

My professor passed away. It is so hard to believe that he is gone. A lovely man, a very good friend, he took me under his wing . . . became like a father to me when I was in university, and at the time, my own father had died . . . .

Things are hectic here. I'm feeling bit overwhelmed with moving. Will not be able to write for a few weeks. Will ring you. Let me know when.

JX

From: Abigail <Abigail@sympatico.ca>
Subject: Glad
Date: 8 March 2012
To: Jenya <Jenya@hotmail.com>

Jenya,

Thanks for the phone call. I'm really glad we connected. There is no rush to type back. I know you are busy. Take your time and write when you can. I hope all goes exceptionally well with your move.

XO,
Abi

From: Abigail <Abigail@sympatico.ca>
Subject: Easter
Date: 14 April 2012, 8:28:31 PM EDT
To: Jenya <Jenya@hotmail.com>

Jenya,

I hope that things are going exceptionally well for you, that you fully enjoyed celebrating Easter and, if in the midst of moving, that you are almost at the fun part—setting up everything new! Making Easter dinner and brunch here was its usual preparation-plan-ahead, welcome-guests enjoyment . . . green-bud sunny, four wheeling, and my walks by the river were deeply welcome fresh air, perspective-offering perfect . . . . That was all until Sunday when just after eating the golf course Easter buffet, George went out to meet his friends for their golf game. Our friends did not arrive. The father had died in a car accident the night before. He is still in shock, not processing the unfathomable. My young George came back into the clubhouse crying. The funeral was today. I thought of your grief for your friend and professor. The same sudden, unexpected loss . . . a jarring, silencing reminder of the brevity of our time. This man was fifty years old. He leaves his wife and three children. He was our attorney.

Jenya, when I make a meal for the dining room, I always hope to instill some thinking into my children so that it is not just the china dishes and ham dinner that they sit up for but some memorable meaning amidst it. This Easter, I had taught them a lesson from the Christian tradition, a quote in Ephesians about "the manifold wisdom of God purposed for us in Christ." I used this verse and simply strung together three words for my children to remember: star, stone, step. Mentioning Bible stories where the Christian God hung a star in the sky above Mary's infant son. He rolled the gravestone away from the empty tomb, and he did this with manifold wisdom so that we could one day step onto streets of gold. Jenya, I taught my children this brief phrase, stringing together only three words . . . about the Christian faith. The day before my twelve-year-old son stood waiting on the first golf tee for a man, he knew well who did not arrive. He had already taken the step. He was dead. I needed the very reminder that I had just taught my children—a reminder of a sovereign who purposes in manifold wisdom, who in the Christian tradition hung a star in the sky, rolled a gravestone away, and will reach out his hand for us as we each one day step into eternity.

Sending love,
Abi

From: Jenya <Jenya@hotmail.com>
Subject:
Date: 24 April 2012
To: Abigail <Abigail@sympatico.ca>

I'm glad you had a good Easter.

JX

Sent from my BlackBerry® wireless device

From: Abigail <Abigail@sympatico.ca>
Subject:
Date: 25 April 2012
To: Jenya <Jenya@hotmail.com>

A good Easter? Oh, your note made me crack up laughing. And laughter was exactly what I needed today.

Much love,
Abi

May 10, 2012

Dear Jenya,

I sat in the seventh row from the front, on the right side, close to the
middle aisle today. The church was large but plain, and I thought of
our "less is more" agreed appreciation. They showed pictures on a
wide screen at the front above the piano. Music played, and Charles's
friends spoke.

Much love,
Abi

June 1, 2012

Dear Jenya,

It's down-pouring, lashing rain here in Canada today. I love the huge splashing drops and hope the thrill of it lasts at least three days! It was a good reason to don my bright orange J.Crew raincoat this morning. Hood up and running through drops, I am so thankful for this day, Friday, June first. One more day to live. I'm aiming to live it fully well. We had so little snow in Canada this past winter that it left us with a shockingly dry spring. The river behind our house that usually rushes in March ice-melting torrents flooding the whole ravine is now only a calm trickle. Because the water is low, I've been able to take the boys down the hill to the trails after school. George loves riding his mountain bike through the forest along the trails while I hike. I can smell the rich, dark-shaded earth under my boots and hear the slow trickle of the river beside us. He pedals ahead of me, his almost man-boy grin beaming in happy exertion. Now and then, he circles back along the trail to find me walking, just checking in to see if I'm OK, although I'm in the ravine with him to make sure he is safe, not yet giving him free ride on his own. As my son rides and I hike, the trees arch gracefully, protectively above our heads over the trail in front of us, and I look ahead at the sunlight streaming intermittent beams through the leafy canopy. I have always walked forward and always forced myself to look ahead, with the exception of this spring.

This spring, you stopped me in my boot-hiking tracks. Jenya, you forced me to look back, and when I did, I saw the trees that arched above my childhood head. I stopped, relived, and remembered.

The arched trees of my childhood path were the only protection I had. But today, it's a beautiful circle—I'm hiking along the trails to ensure safety for my boy, but he is circling back to double check on me. It is a beautiful, mountain-bike-trail-riding, caring mother-son circle. My eldest son has grown in heart-lurching leaps before my eyes. My daughter's toddler ringlets are now twisted up into a golden-tinged pile on her cheerful teenage head. And my youngest strong-boned, blue-eyed competitive one is as tall as I am. I know you share the same feeling of awe and amazement at the same kind of changes in your children. Your two sons have grown so fast. The babies you rocked have become tall high school-graduating, almost men.

I'm looking forward to seeing your sons at the cottage this summer. Send them around the bay. You know my cottage door is always open.

Must go for now. It is time to step out into the rain again. The lovely thing about a downpour is that all the colours shine brighter when wet. It's a welcome-refreshment kind of a day while running through deep puddles and peeking out from under my orange J.Crew hood.

Love,
Abigail

June 2, 2012

Dear Jenya,

I hope your day has begun well, with a cup of spiced ginger tea and a calm, collect-your-thoughts moment.

I thought of you last night as I attended an Opportunity International meeting. My friend Laura hosted it at her home, showing us pictures of her recent trip to Rwanda and giving information about the organization she is supporting. It is very well organized, as the group steps into struggling countries and offers small business loans primarily to women in order to enable them to begin earning income. They have had success helping women break the cycle of poverty and feed and send their children to school. Jenya, the videotaped testimony of these smart, beautiful women's stories was fully inspiring. Their smiles were glowing. I could see the red earth of Africa and feel the heat of the sun on their backs as they built their small businesses. Each lady paid back her loan and had successfully changed her life and the lives of her children. I know you have seen this firsthand and have felt the surge of emotion overflowing that comes with making life better for others.

I love reading about the leprosy villages you've worked in and so appreciate when you send updates on your work. Isn't that exactly what life is about? Seeing the needs of others around us and meeting them to the best of our ability.

Today I can't help but see the screaming silent needs of women right here. Western women in traditionally religious cultures who are encouraged to marry young—they are allowed little or no education then promptly walked to the altar celebrated and married, some as young as eighteen. Living at the intermittent mercy of their husbands, men who have been taught that they have God-given authority over their brides. In the traditional marriage structure, young girls have no personal income, raise babies, and tend to their homes. Jenya, this falls apart when the eighteen-year-old girl, now a mother to three or four children, grows up in this—a strict, cement cultural structure that allows no room and gives no permission for her development. There is no concept that she would have personal goals; she has been taught and often reminded to fully erase herself for the sake of her family.

Her religious parents cannot fathom why she would be unhappy. After all, she has a husband, a house, and children. If she is bored, she is told to clean her house again, fold more laundry, or arrange her spices in alphabetical order. If she is discontent, she is reminded to pray. Yes, can you imagine the screaming silent needs of this girl? Hers is a religiously imposed poverty of purpose. If her husband is a good, patient, kind, and fair man, she can function very well under his authority. However, if he is not, this young girl needs but sees no escape.

A daughter within an extremely fundamental sheltered religion does not know what she is getting into when she vows before God to marry her second cousin. Rather, she follows what she has been taught to believe is the right way, the most godly and moral choice. Imagine now, twenty years later, her silent scream. It is a painful scream that is silenced by her fear of the vow that she unwittingly made.

A life-changing decision made too young, uninformed with little life experience.

If only the pink cement box that these girls are placed in had breathing windows, there would be room enough to grow. There are no windows in the cement walls of chauvinism. It is similar to the slow death of the nation trapped in fear under a tyrannical ruler. Is a nation willing to risk the lives of its sons and daughters for freedom? Likewise, is a mother willing to alter the lives of her young children to break out of the cement walls of her life?

As a child, I lived with the consequences of my mother's breaking out, and as an adult, I am watching my sister-in-law's decision unfold before my eyes. Jenya, Christian girls encased in a culture of extreme fundamentalism risk death.

Not as Muslims who physically take the lives of their daughters that disobey. The Christian death is a living kind of a death, a long, unstoppable daily cruelty. It is the way that extreme Christians distribute their penalty. It is a social death by shunning. I know the slow death; I watched my young mother lose her life to it, and I endured it as a child.

Jenya, today on this rainy day is the time to start typing my survival story, to paint you this life-giving painting. So from time to time, my dear friend, I will slip into Starbucks, open up my very own tiny MacBook Air, and write to you. I delight in this magic silver thing; bought with secretly saved grocery money, my slim computer is privately hidden in my off-white canvas painting class bag.

My heart beat very fast as I walked along the sidewalk from the bank to the small computer store. I had taken my extra grocery money savings out of my account, tucked it into my wallet, and opened the door of the bank. I retraced my steps to the little store where I had, only fifteen minutes before, scoped out the various sizes of computers. I chose this tiny, slim one. It doesn't take a disk, but it does take a memory stick, and it has an apple on it. That it would fit unnoticed into my canvas painting bag and the number of dollars I would give them was about all I needed to know. The young sales techie politely covered his surprise when I paid for my treasure with a stack of cash and asked him to set the thing up into word-working order. I was shaking a little but not nearly as much as I shook when, six months earlier, I went into the bank and opened my own account.

My shaking French-manicured fingers held a documented birth certificate, proof of who I was. The bank lady looked at me steadily. She held my gaze. She told me that I was doing nothing wrong and that it was a good thing for me to have my own bank account. I gulped, forced back the tears that were brimming, and knew deep inside myself that it was not wrong to save my own money. I wanted one thing: to be able to write my painting to you in private. So today, my French-manicured white Western-girl fingers type on a slim silver Apple secret. I paint letters to you, my dear friend.

By now your cup of spiced ginger tea has been enjoyed and your day well started.

Much love,
Abigail

September 3, 2012

Dear Jenya,

It is the end of the first week of back-to-school fall routine. You know the feeling of getting everyone organized and ready for a new school year. Shoes, gym clothes, backpacks, pencils, pens, erasers, and rulers.

It is an excited, apprehensive feeling all bundled into one—the first day of school. I know your boys both began new schools. I so hope their first week went well, that they have confidence stepping into university and high school, fitting in their new dorms and new teams. My heart is with your boys as it is with mine, wanting the very best for them and praying for strength, courage, and protection as they walk ahead. Youth has so much potential. These smart, handsome boys have the ability to study hard, to train on their athletic teams, and to become leaders who make a substantial difference, a solid contribution to their generation. The future for these sons of ours is full of promise. If we can gently guide, consistently support, listen, uphold, and encourage, they will make it, Jenya. These boys will reach their full potential, and we will cheer them on together. There is beauty in that, an unnamed beautiful gift. Not only do we give our sons life, we also help to shape it. Oh, may I shape these tassel-haired boys into well-mannered, excellent men who speak well, lead well, learn well, and walk well. Of course, in order to do any of this, they will have to be able to make decisions, they will need to develop a character that can bravely handle deep difficulty, they will need a resilience that is steadfast and unshaken, and they will need a clear sense of justice and an assurance of truth intertwined with immediate integrity. Yes, that does sound like a lot to develop in these sons at the same time providing a solid base and upholding encouragement for our daughters.

Our mother-daughter group met once a month with a lesson to teach the girls, a theme, and a fun activity to do together. It has been seven years since we began when the girls were nine years old. The New

York City trip was envisioned four years ago. We decided, when the girls turned sixteen years old, to take them to New York City. Jenya, it happened. Just this past Sunday, we flew back from realizing the group-travel dream for these girls. I am completely and wholeheartedly thankful that the goal to walk alongside, encourage, teach, and uphold our daughters has, in the past seven years, taken shape and now been celebrated by this fantastic trip to the city. I'm overflowing with amazement at what has unfolded from my quick, uninformed pick of the red-covered book on the toy store shelf! There are eight other mother-daughter groups organized now. Mother's have started with their eight—and nine-year-olds, aiming for the same goal: to support, encourage, teach, and raise these beautiful girls up well.

No one knows my very likely subconscious motivation for this girls' group, a group in which these girls can feel comfort and belonging and experience fun. A group where they are supported, encouraged, and developed. Today, these young girls have each other because years ago, a tiny child lacked.

Today, after flying back from a mother-daughter trip, I paint letters to you in rich-coloured oils. These are the shades of a fair haired child, the shades of her life painting of peace.

Much love,
Abigail

September 17, 2012

Dear Jenya,

The shades of my painting were found amidst the rain of my childhood suffering when the puddles of sadness were dangerously deep and even the rivers overflowed. It was in the well of wet suffering that I learned to look below the surface and find my coping colours.

This summer, the lake was glassy calm not only in the early morning hours that it would normally be so. The lake was glassy calm all day, from sunrise to sunset, for almost the entire two months. It made for an invigorating, life-balancing, Carl-Douglas-sleek, calm-surfaced wooden sculling. As I complete my row each morning and walk from the glass lake up the stone step to the kitchen to make my morning cup of tea, I look forward to reading the headlines. I skim over the well-written news articles and linger over journalists' words, as though I have the ability right in my own teacup to change everything that upsets me in the news.

On these glass-lake days, I long for peace in Syria. Oh, Jenya, every day I look for the most recent written update. What appears to be is not always the case. Don't just look at the surface of the water; look into it. When I row very early each summer morning, I take a moment to set my posture. Before turning to look over my shoulder and glance at my route, I stop to look into the water. I peer as deep down as I can see into its clear blue-green lake glory. It is so very important to look beyond the surface. On the surface, it does appear that Asma supports the Syrian military regime in which her husband is the president of. Is Omani Rose controlled by fear, intimidation, and humiliation? Required, despite any of her own thoughts, to stand publicly beside her husband? I do not know the answers to these questions, but the questions flow when one looks below the surface. Maybe she does not have her secret MacBook Air; it is possible that she did not save her own grocery money in time.

Surface lookers are like my recent summer cottage guest. The man that stood himself on our dock looked at me, sighed, and said, "It must be great to do nothing all summer." I smiled. Oh, Jenya, I was, at the time, standing calmly in front of him. However, I had, in the previous two days, washed linens, made thirteen beds, planned the full menu for two families for four days, and bought, carried in, and unpacked groceries. I had washed and folded ten red-and-white-stripped striped dock towels, tidied up the dock, ensured the garbage was in the bin and extra sunblock on hand. I checked the wood boxes, made a salad, soaked the cedar planks for fish dinner that night, and counted heads of my own and the various cottage-bay children running in and out. Did I love doing it? Yes. I loved it all and am completely thrilled when the children's craft cupboard was once again filled with supplies that I had prethought through, chosen, and packed from the city for another summer. But the laughing truth of the matter is that this guest, and possibly many others, will come and go from the cottage, having had a full four-day holiday, believing that because the hostess is standing beside a lake, she does nothing all summer. Do you think it would have been impolite to put both of my hands squarely on his chest and launch the man fully clothed into the lake? I know you are doubled over laughing about this because you cottage too, and you know exactly what I mean by ensuring everything functions well, all while complying with the pressure to look cute, relaxed, and like, oh yes, I do nothing all summer. My sanity in the tending to cottage needs and sincerely welcoming guests in an exhausted run is found by reading the newspaper. I remind myself of the utter privilege and the undeserved honor it is to live in Canada. A country built on democracy that many soldier's fought and died for. A nation that offers clean drinking water, access to medical care, a well-rounded education, and freedom of speech. In a country that educates its children and has an established rule of law, I will happily wash dock towels, plan meals, and make dinners for as many adults and children that join in, welcomed around my cottage harvest table. I love the setting, I do not mind the work, and I always, always look below the surface of the water.

My surface today looked lovely and very perfect. It is a sunny September morning. The kind of day where the sun streams across the fields and through the trees, making the leaves glow golden. The smell of fall is just touching the air but not overpowering the warm, ripe bright red tomatoes laden on their bending vines in the garden. Boston ivy has wound its lush, gracefully clinging way up the stone walls, giving green life to the gray and thrill to me as I marvel at its beauty.

After another summer, we have now moved from the cottage back to the city. My painting studio is on the upstairs floor of my gray stone house. Up the spiral wooden staircase, across the wrought-iron-lined bridge, the first door on the right takes you into what was the nursery. Its dark, hard, wooden floors had each of my three babies crawling on them. The tall ceiling has a simple wrought-iron chandelier hanging from it, framed by tall bay windows. Daylight streams warmth in the windows. The walls are painted a pale yellow, ensuring a completely calm background in which to display my latest oil painting on its easel. The desk was my mother's antique Duncan Phyfe table. The wooden bookshelf towering above my head is the one my husband had delivered as a gift. It is filled with copies of Byron, Tennyson, Steinbeck, and Dickens—rows of my favorites, some that you have recommended.

I love the room not only because it was my babies' room, the one in which I cuddled, nursed, and rocked each infant to sleep in, the room that I went to each night, the room in which they greeted me each morning with rosy-cheeked baby smiles with arms outstretched. I love the room because it is my hard-fought-for space.

Now I have my very own beautiful, light-streaming-in studio space. The painting on my easel in my studio now is one for my sister. It is a birthday gift for my only smart, beautiful older sister, a painting of a little girl running forward. Darkness is lifting as she skips toward the light, her arms outstretched, her white skirt flowing. Today I worked on the details of painting the ribbon fringe at the bottom of the little girl's skirt. Hidden in the Moroccan-style ribbon fringe, I will paint golden words. Strengthening words of blessing as both my sister and the little girl in the painting run forward in life.

Today I was practicing the letters for the fringe, contemplating the most empowering, encouraging blessing that I could paint in the picture. Hidden messages in the bottom fringe of a skipping girl's skirt. If only we had words of courage painted on the hem of our skirts each day. Imagine how different a day could be, a day grounded in empowering courage.

I am currently trying to encourage hope in the horrible for my sister. My intelligent, smart only sister whose phone calls lately are distressing and who I'll see tomorrow. I can't wait to make the drive back to the village where I grew up only because my sister still lives there. In this village, the same ferry in which my mother was a single mother, now my only sister is recently a single mother. I can't help but feel huge concern and utter distress when I think of how the same village people will respond now thirty years later. Will the social treatment be the same as it was then?

This is why I am painting her a special canvas, one that shows darkness lifting and light shining. One with power words painted in gold on the hem of a girl's white skirt. It is this close, upholding, courageous, linked arms in love that will allow us to run forward together in overcoming strength, celebration, and victory. In the midst of more tragedy, of more brokenness, of more pain, we link arms again and find strength enough to survive.

My sister and I have been sending each other songs. We call it our *song of the week*. Music that we take turns choosing, which we agree is our shared encouragement for seven numbered days. This week she chose the song "10,000 Reasons" by Matt Redman. Last week, we listened to "Whom Shall I Fear" by Chris Tomlin, and seven days prior to that, our song title was "White Flag."

Sometimes the song we choose is serious; other times it is fully upbeat and makes us laugh.

So tomorrow, my friend, I will drive for four hours with three things: abounding love for my sister, a painting of a girl wearing a skirt with a ribbon fringe hem framed for her wall, and the assurance that in life, one can find hope and healing after what is horrible. I packed my raincoat, just in case. Because I know about water—it either refreshes or drowns.

Much love,
Abigail

September 25, 2012

Dear Jenya,

My life has been painted in terrible, beautiful complimentary shades of colour. In each shade of life experience, there has been a secret childhood lesson learned and a silent principle proven. It was like raindrops falling on old stone, bringing out vibrant shades of taupe and white and gray. I needed sovereign-given girlhood resilience to stand in the rain, and it required forced insight to find the colours and to see below the surface. It was then, my dear friend, that the terrible became beautiful. Because that is the way I choose to paint it.

Much love,
Abigail

The rain to the wind said,
"You push and I'll pelt."
They so smote the garden bed
That the flowers actually knelt,
And lay lodged—though
not dead.
I know how the flowers felt.

—Robert Frost

After the rain and below the surface . . .

Hawthorne Yellow

Had I told you about the killdeer plover's nest?

An excellent life is not a life that knows no danger; an excellent life is one in which we've designed our own nest of safety.

> Out of this nettle, danger, we pluck this flower, safety.
>
> —William Shakespeare

> The door to safety swings on the hinges of common sense.
>
> —unknown

> Say No to all oppression, weather it rise from those you love or from an enemy . . . you will carry shame and self hatred for not resisting—that is worse by far.
>
> Each of us has the right to live without fear. They hold you hostage but call it love.
>
> —Shauna Singh Baldwin, The Tiger Claw

October 9, 2012

Dear Jenya,

It was in a ferry with only two buildings built by the water—one called
the Rideau Ferry Inn and the other, a convenience store gas bar. Both
buildings are located at the foot of the bridge by the water. Various
houses, from shacks to bungalows, are scattered intermittently along
the country road that winds in either direction from the bridge. Old
redbrick, forest green, white-shuttered-veranda farmhouses grace the
rolling green pasture hills. There are small cemeteries dotting the land,
a final resting place for the hardworking farmer, his baby who died
in infancy, his wife lost to cancer, and his father, the one who taught
him respect for and tilled the new land before him. The beauty of this
fertile valley-land is in the generations who have walked its country
roads, the well-worn hands that held quilts delicately stitched and
rolling pinned rolled-out dough to bake golden flaky pies. Simple souls
who sung heart-warming old hymns while raising happy tree-climbing
children. It all, all speaks of a simple life—free from city stress, void of
high demands, looming deadlines, expensive fashion, and maxed-out
overachievers. This place, this little ferry is a tiny hamlet, a haven of
country living highlighted by an afternoon boat ride under the bridge
and a home-cooked meal. It was here, Jenya, that I lived below the
surface and that I learned to paint in my mind the colours that I saw.
In this lush country setting, I survived what was brutal. It was in this
ferry that the terrible became beautiful and in this setting that by a
sovereign hand, my child's mind was preserved.

As I walked from the bus stop at the end of the winding gravel road
to my grandparents' home beside the lake, I thought to myself during
those before—and after-school walks. The sun streamed across the
hawthorne yellow fields. It cut sharp lines through the tall rows of
ripe corn. It landed its hot beams on the yellow dust road at my feet.
I walked step by step, taking in the smell of the fields, listening to the
birds. What kept me walking was the bird at my feet. Called a killdeer
plover, this brown-and-white-feathered bird would feign a broken wing

in order to distract its predator and protect its young. Brilliantly, this bird made its nest in the ground, its eggs camouflaged to look like the stones that surrounded its ground nest. My little bird friend would come out each day that I walked by; my seven-year-old self tried to tell the little mother that I would never harm her or her eggs, but that she did not understand. She would flap and flutter along the ground, trying to distract me. It amazed me why she would choose to nest in the ground. Well, if she could do it, if she could nest in the ground, then so can I. I could blend right in, camouflage myself right into the ground. And so I tried.

They often looked right through me anyway. They looked over my head or in scorn right at me. They wouldn't let their children play with me, have me to their homes, eat with me, shake my hand and, some of them, to speak to me. Of course they wouldn't; I was Gwendolyn's youngest daughter. And that made me shunned just like her. At seven I felt the weight of this life; I felt the need to blend safely into the ground. The killdeer plover found safety there and so could I. *I'll just build a nest in the ground*, I told my seven-year-old self. This bird survives, and while all the other birds are nesting up high, she chooses the ground. I wonder if they ever fly down to visit her. It's such a far distance from the ground to the treetop. I felt the warm sun; the dusty road made little puffs around me as I walked. The dust clung to and covered my navy blue saddle shoes. I smelled the tall dried corn and walked alone down the winding road toward the lake into the comfort of Grandma's arms. Grandma, who too was shunned for taking us in, for helping her daughter. When pain is beyond enduring, Jenya, when people force you down, down so low that you fear you will not survive. When they look past you, through you, and over your head. When they ignore you, discount you, and treat you as dead. When life is mind-crushing, heartbreaking hard. Then, it is then that you make your nest in the ground. They pushed me low, but what they didn't know was that I could build a small hidden, camouflaged place of safety.

At seven years old, when the hurt was far beyond what my mind and heart could bare, I proved this works. It was very simple. I copied the killdeer plover. They made me a no one, a nothing, a dead-to-them girl. So I found safety. In my mind, I copied the killdeer plover; I made my nest in the ground. If I could survive in my low-ground nest of hidden, camouflaged, invisible safety, then one day, I determined I might well use my wings to fly far away from this ferry.

An excellent life is not a life that knows no danger; an excellent life is one in which we've designed our own nest of safety.

Much love,
Abigail

Navy Blue

Had I told you about my blue leather saddle shoes?

An excellent life is not one that has never experienced cruelty; it is a life where one chooses to walk in compassion despite what is cruel surrounding them.

> *You must not lose faith in humanity. Humanity is an ocean; if a few drops of the ocean are dirty, the ocean does not become dirty.*
>
> —Gandhi

> *And let thy feet millennium's hence be set in the midst of knowledge.*
>
> —Alfred Lord Tennyson

October 13, 2012

Dear Jenya,

I'd love to hear how your boys are doing, what their new schools are like. I think of them often and know you are looking out well for them each day.

If it is possible to describe a day in one colour, then today was a navy kind of a day. You know, the kind of fall day where you just feel there is no going back. Warm weather won't have its comfort peek out again this year. Fall has fallen all navy around us, with no warm golden rays until next spring. We are in cool winter colours of this Canadian winter landscape. Navy shoes must be worn, flip-flops tucked away in the closet, for now, replaced. I owned a pair of navy leather saddle shoes, and as a child, they were my favorite. My saddle shoes were very well worn-out, both with cracked soles. The leather was thick navy, soft but strong. These navy leather childhood shoes walked my feet from home to school and to meeting. Both soles of my shoes were broken right across the bottom, but no one could tell. So I kept wearing them. Navy matches almost every outfit, and my shoes carried me to the little yellow building. It had once been a one-room redbrick building with a wood stove in the middle. At some point, the men decided to build what they called a new hall. So that is where the meetings were held, in the yellow-sided building with bare, plain walls, a few windows, and old wooden seats.

They called it the *Meeting*. They didn't believe in naming themselves. However, when you refuse a name, others still need to categorize your group; so others called them the Exclusive Plymouth Brethren. And there they were, a group of maybe 120 of them. Well, eighty of them in the ferry but more in the two surrounding towns over. If there were Bible meetings held with a meal, it was called a fellowship tea. All three assemblies would get together and invite others connected to the same group to join in for special meetings. Homemade food would be displayed on two long tables in the back of the hall, a selected speaker would teach after the meal, and people would chatter and visit. The men would visit about farming, local business, and narrow theology; the women would chatter about quilting, weddings, and babies.

If you looked at the surface, the pie was homemade tasty, the casseroles were home-baked delicious, fresh garden-grown salads were colourful and varied, the coffee and tea were served by ladies wearing hats. Of course, we had to cover our heads by wearing hats, lace veils, or tams. One of these choices had to be on our girl heads to cover our hair, which they taught was our glory. Our long skirts were either floral or denim, our sweaters or blouses always modest. The most thrilling of Sundays was, of course, the days when we would dress a little fancy with our Laura Ashley floral dresses and white petticoats. I liked my Laura Ashley dress; it was expensive and could only be bought in the city. My sister's dress matched mine in style, and we wore wide-brimmed straw hats to go with our special dresses.

It would have been sunny-country, happy special for some, the ones who were *gathered*. If you were gathered, you belonged at the table. That meant when they passed communion, a loaf of unbroken fresh bread and a cup of wine, you got to take a piece of bread and sip from the cup of wine as they were passed around the room. Four squares of chairs sat facing the middle where the handmade lace cloth-covered table stood, with the plate of bread and glass cup of wine on it. I watched them pass both the bread and the wine around each Sunday morning. I watched as they drank from the cup and picked off a small piece of bread. I watched and dangled my legs over the edge of the wooden seat. My feet didn't touch the floor. My legs weren't long enough to sit up straight ladylike and touch the floor with my navy shoes. So they dangled. I tried to cross my legs like the older girls. It didn't work for long. I'd get a stitch in my hip, as my grandma called it. That meant a pain in my back. The hard wooden chair and my attempt to be grown-up ladylike—unable to touch the floor with my toes—did not go well together. So I'd dangle my seven-year-old legs, my feet tied neatly into my navy leather shoes with little white ankle socks, swinging. I sat at the very back of the room, in the two rows of chairs set out for those "not in fellowship."

I was sure not in. They made that clear. We were shunned. My grandpa, my grandma, my mother, my sister, and I all sat in the back row. Not allowed, of course, to sit with the congregation. I, the youngest, sat in the back, at seven. The rules were made clear by a letter that the Brethren wrote to my mother. They pushed the letter under the door at my grandpa and grandma's house. The letter told her that she was out of fellowship, that she could attend the meetings on Sundays, but she was to sit at the back and not take a piece of passed-around bread or sip the passed-around cup of wine. She was not to eat with the congregation and not to shake anyone's hand. The letter, pushed by some man under the wooden front door, made my mother officially shunned.

During the eleven years of shunning, there were two people who were able to step over the threshold of the front door and into Grandma's home. One, a balding, simple but sincere man, the other a smart, strong but tiny lady. The balding painter whose Irish accent coupled with his local valley twang gave him almost a dialect all his own. He was hired to paint interior walls, to glue blue floral wallpaper up in the bedroom, and generally, to do odd jobs around Grandpa and Grandma's lake house. Grandpa's brain tumor surgery had left him paralyzed on one side. He had recovered his speech but, whose heavyset gait needed a cane and left him dragging his left foot—a very noticeable limp.

This meant a man with more agility was needed to do the physical man work. Our balding painter was a chatterer, and on the days he was there, which were many because he took a very long time doing a job and was paid by the hour, his Irish valley chatter filled the kitchen. And he was not too proud or too religious to take a cup of tea and a snack that Grandma offered him each day. That he would eat in Grandma's kitchen was so shocking for us and risky for him that we never spoke of it outside the house. My mom and grandma often nodded to each other as he'd sit his cheerful self down for a slice of homemade cake. His chattering brought the village gossip; it livened Grandma's day, and although she laughed as though she tired of it, he was the only one person of two who, for years, stepped through Grandma's front door. We had the chatting painter and spritely Gladys.

This tiny cheerful strength would come to Grandma's house once every few months, as often as it is that a lady needs a home permanent hair do. A Toni, they called the bottles of strong-smelling solution, sold in a box. It was a seriously exciting and special day; the one that Gladys would come to Grandma's to have her hair done. The house was cleaned the day before. I was told that "Gladys was coming," which meant that I could peek into the bathroom where the activity was, but I was not to interrupt. It was on Gladys days that strong ammonia filled the upstairs and wafted down the hallways. The cream rise was a special part because that was put on her tiny, frame, silver white hair after the job was done, and various sizes of wire bristle curlers were then nestled in neat rows, stuck in place with pink plastic sticks. The hair dryer was a puffed-out plastic hat-like thing that went on Gladys's head. It was so loud that no talk could be heard above it, but the ladies raised their voices anyway for a few brief sentences over and above the puffed-out-hat, plastic-hose-attached hair dryer noise. I watched this lovely, happy process as I peeked around the corner of the door. Grandma did this as Gladys sat on the wicker stool facing the large mirror. They looked at each other in the big bathroom mirror, the one that I had been asked to shine with Windex for the special occasion. Together, the ladies reminisced, as they had been longtime friends; and on those days, I heard Grandma laugh. Her blue eyes shone and she relaxed for a moment, amidst the smell of the home permanent and with Gladys, whose intelligent plan worked. She must have convinced them that of all the village ladies, it was her best friend Hilda who was needed to do her hair. Jenya, a tiny gray-haired lady outsmarted them. She did it using one small box called a Toni.

The rest of the church-village people went silent. They talked to each other but not to us. They ate meals together, but not with us; they visited, celebrated, socialized, brought meals to each other, but not to us. We were put out. Family Christmases with cousins and aunts and uncles were no longer; Thanksgiving meetings and conferences were no more; fellowship lunches, dinner invitations, wedding celebrations were no longer open for our participation. Anything that included talking to someone or eating with them was, by the power of one letter, no longer part of my mother's or my grandpa and grandma's experience. I was seven years old when that letter was pushed under the door. One powerful and crucial page typed out and signed by six men at the bottom. A letter, one that changed our lives forever.

My navy blue shoes dangled over the edge of the wooden chair. The chair I sat on was in the line of back row chairs. There was a large walking space between the row of chairs placed at the back of the room and the rows of chairs for those who belonged. Some man each Sunday would set up the chairs at the back. He would place the wooden chair that my seven-year-old self would dangle my feet from. Little feet that were punished, disciplined, and put out in shame for my mother's choices. I felt heart-lurching, stomach-churning, nauseating shame. My soul was broken. Broken the same as the sole of my little girl navy blue leather shoes.

My shoes were broken underneath but no one can see. Can anyone see the inside of me broken? Dangle, swing, dangle, swing—my navy shoes clung to my tiny white ankle socks as the people around me sang, "Blessed assurance, Jesus is mine." The pain of sadness in my chest all the way down to my tummy ached deeply and continually. My head hurt. My mommy had left my daddy. She had left her husband and brought her two little girls to this ferry to live with her parents. Said she was "fed up;" that's why she left Montreal, why she hurried her two little girls into the car one unexpected day. That's why I quickly grabbed my dolls. You can carry more dolls if you grab some by their hair. My arms were full of dolls, so Jane and Raggedy Ann were rush carried to the car, their hair squeezed in between my fingers, their bodies dangling, clashing together as I ran. I didn't want to hurt them, but they could not be left behind. They needed to come with me right away.

And so there we were, living at my grandparents' home, my young mother lying in the bed beside me, gasping, sobbing herself to sleep each night. With no marriage counseling, no divorce recovery, no support, no kindness, no understanding, and no help. There we were in an exclusive Brethren community in which divorce was unheard of. There was no precedent for this; here, this young crying woman, her two little daughters, and her parents. Her parents who, at great cost, took her in.

My grandma lost her three other children and grandchildren. She lost her lifelong friends. She lost the only sense of community she had ever had. Because she took her daughter in, they all refused to talk to her; they treated her as though she were dead.

Years later, as I was helping Grandma dig beside the holly hocks in her garden, I asked her, "Grandma, you don't believe in divorce, but you took us in. Why did you do it?" "Oh dear," Grandma said, "when you have a daughter and your daughter comes to you in trouble, you will help her." She answered with no hesitation. No hesitation, Jenya. My grandma took her daughter into her home, with social death to her own self. And she was completely clear—sure of why she did it. Swing, dangle, swing. I wonder if my toes, in my navy shoes with my white ankle socks rolled over, will ever be able to reach the floor. As the congregation of self-righteous, staring-at-me people sang "How Great Thou Art," I could hear the sounds of my mother's sobbing and feel her body shaking next to me in bed each night.

My mother dressed us well. She took careful time to ensure we had matching *outfits*, she called them. My blond hair got stuck with heat to my forehead. I pushed the strands out of my eyes up under my hat. My dress was pretty, but it was a tiny bit itchy on the day that a perfectly beautiful, very happy chubby girl looked my way. She smiled at me and I smiled back. From then on, I had one friend.

My one and only braided brown-haired, rosy-cheeked little girl confidant lived in town. She was a very far-feeling, twenty-minute drive away. We didn't take the same school bus but crossed paths as we sat beside each other on wooden plank benches. The flat planks were set on top of logs outside under the trees for summertime Sunday school. Her jolly nature, coupled with the fact that our mothers had known each other as teenagers, helped us slip through the cracks of the rules. Unlike the other girls from the meeting who told me flatly that unless my mother went back to live with my father, they could not talk to me, this braided, brown-haired jolly playmate smiled and giggled. She even invited me into her house. I marveled as she showed me the very pretty old tiny rose wallpaper in her upstairs attic farmhouse room. Her giggles bathed my despair and loneliness in intermittent glimpses of girlhood happiness. Her parents were busy, and as the only girl in a rambunctious family of five children, worrying about who she spoke to at Sunday school was not their foremost concern. With this one exception of my in-town giggling little girlfriend, I was not invited to play with the children in this village and, at the same time, was taught to be separate from the "worldly" children at school. I guess that puts me walking where? Where exactly did they expect me to walk? But even as reality of being shunned by the meeting children and the rules to be separate from the schoolchildren crashed around in my dismayed head, during those eleven years, one friend at a time was provided.

At first, my seven-year-old self had the occasional joy of brown-haired, braided, giggling, Sunday school bench-sitting girlfriend confidant. By the time I was sixteen years old, I had met a tall blond girl whose family vacationed in this ferry. She would come to holiday each summer. Since she was from a town six hours away, she didn't seem to fear any consequences of speaking to me and asked me to play tennis with her. I stared at her tall, beautiful self and agreed, with utter bursting joy flooding my shamed self. Of course, I would love to play tennis with her. I would have just loved to stand beside her; even her acknowledgment that I existed was enough, Jenya. She didn't look through me or turn her head away as the other girls did. Her very first kindness to include me in her plans saved my despair-drowning life. In those days, we did not e-mail; instead, we wrote handwritten letters and mailed them back and forth. We confided our secrets and continued to visit each other from time to time as we studied at different universities. Jenya, you've met her as her cottage is close to both of ours. She has stuck close to me all these years.

The third girl stopped into my world briefly. But her brief stopping in was long enough for her to give me a present. The very first present that I ever received from a friend sits in a special place on my desk today. She gave me a book. She wrote in the front cover of it for my seventeenth birthday, one year to the month before I would make my way from the ferry into the city. This down-to-earth girl handed me a green soft-covered book entitled *Streams in the Desert* written by Mrs. Charles E. Cowman. For years, I only noticed the first name *Charles* until reading the *Mrs.* in front of the man's name. Realizing then with awe-flooding surprise that the author's words, the ones which I had been clinging to each morning, reading were penned by a lady. My book-giving friend was in the middle of a high school photography project. Needing a subject, she placed our laughing, teenage girl selves in a green field, and we took each other's pictures. Of course, I wore my red dress for the field picture.

Jenya, each of these three girls were blankets of friendship when I was otherwise completely desolate.

But yes, at seven years old, at twelve years old, and at sixteen years old, while I dangled my legs and looked down at my blue saddle shoes, I learned one thing. Jenya, I learned to never judge another until you have walked a mile in their shoes. Never judge because the person you judge lower than yourself may just have a broken soul. Swing, dangle, swing. You can't see the soles of another person's shoes. They may be hiding more sadness than you could ever imagine; it's possible they don't know where to fit in. Perhaps they are filled with regret from their own mistakes.

Today I am typing to you wearing tall leather boots. Tall ones, the style that come up over the knee; the soles of my boots are worn in from walking, but they are not broken. It has taken time, but healing has been poured in. And I don't drown in puddles of self-pity. I splash in the puddles and give thanks for survival, plain and simple healing survival.

My sole-broken shoes have been mended, and I have learned to walk ahead in tall boots. I walk ahead while at the same time not forgetting the way in which a community of people broke a seven-year-old, fair-haired child's soul.

An excellent life is not one that has never experienced cruelty; it is a life where one chooses to walk in compassion despite what is cruel surrounding them.

Much love,
Abigail

Scarlet Red

Had I told you about my red dress?

An excellent life is not a life that is free from humiliation. An excellent life is a life filled with ironclad hope that triumphs despite humiliation.

> Therefore behold I will allure her, I will speak tenderly to her . . . then I will give her her vineyards from there, and the valley of Achor as a door of hope.
>
> —Hosea 2:14-15

For millennia women have dedicated themselves almost exclusively to the task of nurturing, protecting and caring for the young and the old, striving for the conditions of peace that favour life as a whole. To this can be added the fact that, to the best of my knowledge, no war was ever started by women. But it is women and children who have always suffered most in situations of conflict. Now that we are gaining control of the primary historical role imposed on us of sustaining life in the context of the home and family, it is time to apply in the arena of the world the wisdom and experience thus gained in activities of peace over so many thousands of years. The education and empowerment of women throughout the world cannot fail to result in a more caring, tolerant, just and peaceful life for all.

—Aung San Suu Kyi

October 15, 2012

Dear Jenya,

Our song of the week is "Be Still" by The Fray. As I listened to it today, I read the newspaper headlines today here in Canada are about a fifteen-year-old girl who suffered bullying online and at school and who took her own life.

Last week, the headlines were about a fourteen-year-old schoolgirl, Malala Yousafzai, in Pakistan shot in the head by the Taliban for attending school and blogging under a pen name.

Jenya, young girls are dying today for attending school in the Swat Valley, and young girls are being bullied to their deaths while being educated in schools in Canada. I understand both girls. The headlines catch my attention and I pore over them, drinking in each word of their appallingly painful stories. I understand these girls. I feel Malala's fear. I know the courage she needed to persevere.

When the Brethren taught that it was worldly to play organized sports, I tried out for the high school volleyball team. While the Brethren taught that we were to be separate from the world and not speak to unbelievers, I shyly got to know some girls in my class at school. When the Brethren spoke loudly and clearly that it was unnecessary and ungodly to attend university, I stood my it-is-necessary-for-me ground. I stood my silent ground so much so that when my grandparents told me with guilt pressure not to leave the village because in doing so, I would be leaving my mother in a house to live all alone, I applied for school, found a roommate, and moved to the city. I didn't risk being shot in the head, but I knew firsthand the death of disobedience. Jenya, extreme fundamentalists eliminate people in different ways. Some, like in Pakistan, impart physical death; others, like in this ferry, impart a social death for breaking their rules. They refuse to educate their daughters, have only men in their religious leadership structures, and both claim heaven as the reward for believing, complying with, and obeying the doctrinal rules. They pound closed iron fists on holy books, teaching their god's law and making themselves the strict enforcers of it. Little girls are taught from childhood to be quiet, humble, and submissive. To serve others, esteem others higher than themselves, to erase their desires, and to silence their opinions. For a lifetime, some women are physically confined to their homes, only able, as my grandmother was, to go into town when her husband drove her.

It was a scarlet dress that gave me strength. First, the dress was in the painting hanging on the wall in my grandma's house. The colours in the painting and the story I made up around it fascinated me. The scarlet red dress-wearing little girl had blond ringlets, her pale chubby hand reached up to pet a handsome black dog. I stared at her for hours, hearing the crashing sea behind her, imagining myself dancing on the seashore, running alongside the girl, playing with the dog. I was with her, laughing, chasing, and collecting pretty seashells. In my childhood isolation, the girl in the painting became my friend. She needed no name; on many days, she was the only one I had. Later as a teenager, I begged my mother to buy me my very own scarlet red dress. I wore it with a white crocheted lace petticoat showing beneath the hem as at the time, white petticoats were sold in the same store, displayed on mannequins under all different patterns and colours of dresses.

The scarlet red dress gave me hope. Its colour and style made me, for the first time in my life, wonder if I would ever look pretty. Not as pretty as the girl in the painting but maybe just a tiny-bit-of-a-touch pretty. Shame covered me inside and out, humiliation hovered; loneliness was my life. I was ugly and unwanted.

But, Jenya, my red dress days were scarlet moments of ironclad hope. Hope artesian welled up from under my continual humiliation. Red dress-wearing days were secret hope-fighting-horror days. Maybe I could be pretty even while sitting on the back row of the church. While standing on the sidelines, while watching as the perfectly well-behaved, pale-faced, dark-haired girl sit up to play the piano in front of a roomful of adults at her father's command. She was accepted. She was loved. She was the speaker's special only daughter. I watched the perfect girl from the edge of the crowd. I would never be her; her family would not eat with me. I was Gwendolyn's daughter. I was shunned. But if a scarlet red dress can give a girl courage, this dress did. If two paintings hung side by side can let a girl jump into them, these paintings hanging on my grandma's wall did. They invited my little girl self in. While wearing that scarlet red dress, my silent hope became greater than their given humiliation. A painting of a little girl on the wall, my imaginary playmate, a matching scarlet red dress, and hope. Ironclad hope that did not die.

Rather, it rose up like an unstoppable crashing sea wave in my child's heart, and I learned, Jenya, I learned how to rise above. Rise above it, dear. Rise above it even if you need to wear a scarlet red dress on an extremely brutal and sadly I-am-nothing, lonely day. My preteen, girl-child silent hope rose above their proud, intolerant, unkind, poured-out humiliation.

Years later, when in university, I read Hawthorne's novel, *The Scarlet Letter*. In an old redbrick house, student-rented-out apartment in Canada, relief flooded in rushing torrents into my mind. For the first time ever, in these book pages, somebody had lived like me. Finally, someone understood me. Her novel-reading name was Pearl.

An excellent life is not a life that is free from humiliation. An excellent life is a life filled with ironclad hope that triumphs despite humiliation.

Much love,
Abigail

Lilac Mauve

Had I told you about Grandma's violets?

An excellent life is not one that is reduced to bitterness, an excellent life blooms in the beauty of reality.

> There are moments in our lives, there are moments in a day, when we seem to see beyond the usual. Such are the moments of our greatest happiness. Such are the moments of our greatest wisdom.
>
> —Robert Henri, foreword to The Art Spirit

> Survival lies in sanity and sanity lies in paying attention. My Grandmother knew what a painful life had taught her . . . The quality of life is in proportion, always, to the capacity for delight. The capacity for delight is the gift of paying attention.
>
> —Julia Cameron, The Artist's Way

> I can still feel how my mothers loved me. I have cherished their love always. It sustained me. It kept me alive. Even after I left them, and even now, so long after their deaths, I am comforted by their memory.
>
> —Anita Diamant, The Red Tent

October 17, 2012

Dear Jenya,

It was an early morning drive to take my son to his school volleyball tryouts this morning. Together we drove toward his school and watched the sun rise. "Nature's first green is gold, her hardest hue to hold . . . As dawn goes down to day, nothing gold can stay" came to mind, and we recited the short poem that he had just learned. We actually watched the golden dawn turn to day, and my heart thrilled in the moment. The thrill was not only having my handsome healthy boy beside me in the car but that his hockey-playing, puck-dragging, crossbar-pinging mind could also hold and understand a poem made my day.

I knew as I drove that I would write to you today, and for that, too, I was looking forward. The days when I secretly type to you are the best. I trust you; my letters are our secret, and this makes me feel safe in the telling. This particular Starbucks is the one in which I first began. On that pouring-rain day, I typed to you wearing my orange coat. Today, I am wearing the same orange coat. I figured it was cheerful for a sunny fall day too, and it goes with the little floral print American Eagle skirt that I picked up on sale. My tall boots are an everyday wear, as always. And so before sunrise, I got set for a full but happy day. I plan to bake banana bread after I get my youngest fair-haired, wonderfully humorous boy packed to travel to his hockey tournament and before I go to the high school to watch my daughter's basketball game. You know the feeling, it is an on-the-go run to keep it all functioning. And not only keep it functioning for the children but to do it cheerfully in that Mommy-is-happy-to-be-your-taxi-driver kind of a way. I love being here for my three children, to drive, support, and uphold. To help recite spelling words, to design paper-mache projects, to study for tests with their rapidly learning minds, and to flour sprinkle fresh homemade bake. The days that I whip up sweet potato turkey shepherd's pie or simmer spaghetti sauce are the happiest ones. Flavor fills the cast-iron pot, I cut up fresh green herbs to add to the tomato red sauce, and imagine the healthy goodness of the vegetables gently bubbling their tastes together. Favorites to make and to eat, pots of love that go over well with hungry growing children. Jenya, I utterly love domesticity at its warmhearted homemade best when it is chosen by a grown girl, not forced on an eighteen-year-old child.

But, my dear friend, I will drift back to the well of childhood as I have allowed myself to do. Back to the mauve walls in Grandma's bedroom, a shade of mauve that was not purple and was not gray. It was a floating, soft sky-like mauve. It was a room of calm peace in the midst of deep sadness. It was the place in which my grandma lived. I don't know when she moved into her own room in the house, but so it was she had her own room. Her husband, my grandfather, had his. Their rooms were not side by side; hers was down the hallway. As a child, I didn't question this; however, now as an adult, I see that my grandma had left her husband. In the only way she could, she got as far away from him as possible. She distanced herself from her controlling, questionable-business-activity husband. She saw him for what he was and wanted no part of that character. With no option to actually leave the home, she moved as far away as she could down the hallway.

Grandma's character shone mauve-silver glowing good. My grandma was gracious, poised, well grounded, and gentle. Her silver hair was daily combed out, teased, and coiled up into an immaculate French roll. The front of her hairdo was puffed up in gentle waves, with a touch of curl on one side. It flowed up with a gorgeous white streak winding its way up the curl puff amidst the silver. The height of her French roll depended on the amount of teasing that my mom put in her mother's hair. As Grandma sat on the stool looking into the bathroom mirror, her daughter—my mother—made her mother's hair look freshly professionally done elegant. My grandma's silver French rolled-up fancy hair was enhanced by her kind, clear, intelligent blue eyes. Oh, Jenya, it was her gracious, intelligent kindness that could not be missed. She said very little, of course, having been trained to be silent and submissive. She had been raised on a farm, married quickly to a city man who brought her to Montreal and promptly left her to travel on business. Alone while tending a woodstove, she kept their home warm and raised up four children. In my mother, her second eldest daughter, living within a neglectful and dictatorial marriage, functioning within an extreme fundamentalist religious group, alone and with so few options, my grandma's spirit of kindness and compassion survived. Looking back on her, she had so many justified reasons to be angry. She held many unfulfilled dreams, but bitterness did not touch her. From this grandma's life I learned my lesson in mauve.

Sometimes, rules don't match reality, and when they don't, always choose reality. My grandma knew the strict rules of this cultural group, but her reality was having a distraught daughter arrive on her doorstep with two little girls. Grandma chose reality; she chose me. When she chose, she was fully aware that she was breaking the rules. By taking her daughter into her home, this made her a supportive party to her daughter's separation from her husband. Grandma would live out brutal lifelong consequences. Because of this choice, she lost everything. Her other three adult children and grandchildren refused to speak to her. Old friends turned their backs on her. People on Sunday morning refused to make eye contact. I watched her isolation grow as she tended to her lakeside home bereft of all comfort and any kindness. Grandma diligently made delicious meals and set her breakfast table the night before, her white linen tablecloth neatly sprayed and starch ironed. I helped her lay the fine china, peach rose-painted plates on the table. I put fresh candles in her silver candelabras, and I stood on my tiptoes to help her stir the special egg white-beaten, meringue-covered cradle cake we specially made together. Outside in the fresh air sunshine, I excitedly packed spring melting snow into the square beige plastic dishpan she gave me. Over the white snow, Grandma would pour sticky golden maple syrup from her stove top boiled thick. The candy-dripping sweetness would firm up on the cold snow, allowing my wooden Popsicle stick to cling to its sap-running goodness.

One day, as Grandma looked out over the lake, she pointed out her friends. A pair of loons swam in front of the rocks, as if they were heaven-sent comfort in her abyss of loneliness. In the winter, when the lake was frozen and the ground blanketed with snow, I would open the lakeside door to the frosty air. Out I would step wearing Grandma's coat, pulled on my tiny body, with her floppy-sided, zipped-up old lady boots over my little girl feet. I stepped into the fresh snow to place the bird cake, in a tin foil pan, on the outside table. It was made of sewet, Grandma called it. I had watched her pour hot bacon grease into a tin can and fill it with birdseed. The seeds would stick together in the hardened grease, making the most plump, seedy, cake-like thing. The seed-filled cake drew her friends to the outside table. It brought us welcome company. I got to walk the cake to the white wintery outside, an offering to the blue jays and cardinals, the chickadee's and nuthatches that fluttered in to feast on Grandma's tin can-made treat.

When I was overcome with sadness, she cuddled me on her red sofa, patted my back, and said, "It's OK, my treasure lamb, just cry it out, cry it out, and then you will feel better." Grandma knew I needed to cry out the brutal brokenness of my child life. She knew the injustice, unfairness, the horror, and the consequences of breaking their religious rules. I made it through those days because of Grandma's understanding, insightful comfort. I could dance my little girl bare feet from the mauve walls of Grandma's comforting bedroom down the wide golden carpeted staircase into the kitchen overlooking the lake. In Grandma's kitchen, there was a large sunny-side window. The counter under the side window held a display of tiny pots, and pouring out of the pots were Grandma's African violets.

In all shades of purple and mauve, these delicate little flowers bloomed almost continually. I was allowed to carefully water each plant and to add a white stick of fertilizer to the soil in each pot. Grandma taught me to pinch the base of each finished bloom, removing it and then to wait for the next cluster of buds. Now I see the enjoyment and the hope that these little plants gave. They never disappointed. Their blooms always came. Grandma and I waited for them, marveled at them, and I understood right then. I saw in Grandma's kitchen overlooking the lake that no one, no matter how mean, can take away the bloom. They can take away friends, they can take away family, they can take away freedom, and they can even force you into silence. They can make sadness fall so heavy that it feels like you will die, but even on that heavy, "maybe I'll die of sadness" kind of a day, the African violet still holds its tiny but strong deep mauve head up. Hold your head up, dear. Yes, you are delicate, but no one, no one can stop you from blooming. There is silent secret in that little windowsill plant. Water it, fertilize it, and watch it bloom.

Grandma knew the strength of the African violets. She knew, and she had dozens of them growing on a counter under a plant light, beside a large lake window. Grandma, intelligent, gracious, and kind, chose to walk in reality over obeying their rules. She knew the secret of the African violets bloom held high, and she knew that bitterness is not beautiful. Grandma, in strength and courage before her time, distanced herself as far as she could from bad character. She relied on her own intelligent thought over ingrained church doctrine. A woman much ahead of her time who gave her own life to care for mine. One day, when my hair goes gray, I may just wear it fancied up in a French roll. I will wear my hair up in honor of the gracious lady who said little, saw the truth, and bravely but knowingly sacrificed her own life to save mine.

Jenya, an excellent life is not reduced to bitterness; an excellent life blooms in the beauty of reality.

Much love,
Abigail

Flagstone Gray

Had I told you about my stepping-stones?

An excellent life is not an unbroken life. An excellent life is a life in which one has intelligently assembled secure stepping-stones.

> *Pass into the midst of the Jordan, and take up every man a stone . . . and these twelve stones shall be for a memorial unto the children of Israel forever.*
>
> *—Joshua 4*

> *They are going to visit a stone cutter, who will engrave the mani mantra into stone for them so that they are protected from evil and will prosper.*
>
> *—Xinran, Sky Burial*

> *Oh thou afflicted, tossed with tempest, and not comforted, behold, I will lay thy stones with fair colours, and lay thy foundations with sapphires.*
>
> *—Isaiah 54:11, KJV*

October 19, 2012

Dear Jenya,

I got word yesterday that your boys are doing well. Jenya, I am so happy to hear that. You must be feeling glad too, just to know that they are walking forward one step at a time, becoming the men that you want them to be. Growing up is not an easy, trouble-free task, is it? There are many stepping-stones along the way. I do see a level head on my daughter's shoulders and pray protection over her but know that teenage years are riddled with pitfalls and possible pain. The only positive for me, having been raised in a closed culture in a very small village, was that there was not a huge amount of trouble to get into. Fear of hellfire consequences kept my curiosity at bay. There must have been drugs, but I did not see them. There were teenagers sleeping around, but I did not hear details. Parties were held in farmers' fields and at the quarry, but I did not attend them. So with a severe lack of normal teenage socialization and complete lack of street sense, off I went at eighteen to the cement sidewalks of the city. I was unaccustomed to the busy city; it took a long time to relax while walking the few blocks from my old redbrick house apartment to the university campus. I had forced my way to school with determination that included an argument with my mother and grandparents. They were sure I needed to stay in the village, but I saw no future in that idea. I longed to get out of the town, away from the self-righteous stares of the churchgoers. I was reaching ahead, thirsty to learn. I am sure it was the longing to learn and the longing for more. More than just in this village, living under these religious rules beside these people.

I would, as the old-fashioned saying goes, rather have jumped in front of a train than to get into "trouble" with a boy before I was married. They called it *fornication* and considered it the worst sin right up there with adultery. If you were accused of either, shunning was your sure consequence, and your reputation never recovered. For generations, you'd be long physically dead and people would still whisper about the girl caught in fornication. So kisses with my tall, rosy-cheeked high school-crush boyfriend were just that—sweet, stolen-on-the-cheek pecks that made both of us blush uncontrollably. He would lean over toward me, his lean, lanky boy frame dressed in new Levi's Jeans with a crisp white Ralph Lauren button-down collared shirt. I could smell men's spicy Polo cologne and see the top edge of his T-shirt underneath the white button down. I could feel his nervousness right next to mine. I was both scared and curious about his unfamiliar maleness but felt wonderfully safe in his arms all at the same time. Handwritten notes passed back and forth in class and confided-in conversations soon met the attention and clear disapproval of his parents. His family had their own business in town, were raising two sons and a daughter, and had a reputation to maintain. His being seen with me, Gwendolyn's daughter, would harm them. I was not worthy of their family and should, in no way, be near their son. He was forbidden to see me, breaking my then seventeen-year-old heart with the cruel but real reminder, again, of who they made me to be.

Our secret sneaking-out, bike-ride-meeting moments didn't last long. The tree-lined side road country laneway that we chose to meet on did not hide us well enough. I still remember the feeling of pedaling my bike along the worn gravel stone road. Pushing the pedals of my silver bike down, catching my breath after making it up the gently curved hill, the clumps of daisies, the smell of new tree leaves and spring fields floating across the road in the wind. Someone reported seeing us together, and that was it. My tall, rosy-cheeked teenage boy got in trouble. I don't know exactly what his parents said to their then seventeen-year-old son, but it was enough to crash cold water on the flickering flame of first love. With humiliation again pouring down my head, reminding me that I was not worthy—unlovable, unwanted, and unclean. Years later, while reading a novel set in India and learning about their caste system, I gasped. The *Dalit*. I understand them; I am one of them. Although I am a pale white Canadian girl, I am placed exactly as they are. They are born into their societal place and told that they are low, unlovely, dirty, unwanted. I was an untouchable, so of course, this family did not want me to be near their son.

In our village, my grandparents, my mother, my sister, and I were the only ones put out of the community. In India, there are millions of people living this same unwarranted shame from birth. I did not marry the rosy-cheeked high school boy. How could I knowingly join a family that did not want me? I couldn't.

The stones on that country laneway side road where I biked to meet my secret young boy led to the cement city sidewalk that I excitedly and apprehensively tread to university. My sneaking out along the gravel road became a forced bravery walk on city university-bound sidewalks. I looked at the campus map and was wearing a brand-new, soft white Roots hoodie zipped with the hood up—my shelter against the fall wind. By myself I found the right cement building, stepped up the steps, and in my mind, repeatedly matched the room number on the top edge of the door frame to the number on my printed-out class list. I sighed in anxious relief as I chose a seat in what I hoped was the correct lecture room. The girls beside me wore stylish city boots, their hair was done in a city fashion, and they wore makeup. My long hair tangled itself in windblown waves, and I had only ever seen pictures of Revlon and CoverGirl. It was ungodly to paint your nails in colour or, even far worse, to colour your lips and face. So I sat in my first university lecture with an unpainted face, noticing that the city girls around me looked rather stunning with their eyes outlined and thinking that maybe CoverGirl had the right idea.

The small gravel stones became the cement sidewalk that eventually led to the pieces of stone that I watched being laid while building a flagstone cottage walkway. One step leads on to another. "Yet knowing how way leads on to way, I doubted if I should ever come back," Robert Frost describes it in *The Road Not Taken*.

Life, Jenya, can be so obviously broken—shattered dreams, shattered hearts, shattered families, lives, minds, and souls. But the broken, Jenya, can become the best. One stone can be placed alongside another. Stones can be arranged in a logical pattern. When one stone is placed beside another and another is laid beside that, a flagstone walkway is built. It is the most solid and secure footed pathway that winds its way forward. The very hard work is required when placing the stones. It is psychological, logic-faith-straining effort to arrange the broken pieces of our lives to fit together. This logical building forward can be done with the broken pieces of our lives.

For me, the country round gravel stone road led me to the cement city sidewalk and then to a flagstone cottage pathway. I looked back and saw each of my stones. Along the way of my life, there had been crucial moments of suffering. Suffering stone moments that I have survived. Each time, I imagined myself picking up a stone in the middle of the river. Just like the Israelites were told to do. At the scariest place in their journey, they were asked to stop when they would rather have wanted to run. They were instructed to pick up and carry something heavy when they would rather have lessened their weight in order to get to the other side sooner. Jenya, I took each picked-up, suffering-stone moment from my life and logically fitted the stones of remembrance side by side. When I laid the broken stones together and then looked at them from above, my suffering stones became a flagstone pathway. I realized, when I arranged the stones of difficulty logically to fit together, Jenya, I could build a secure way forward.

Even through challenging, pressure-filled, figuring-out-life years, our teenagers can take each step. They can be taught how to place the broken pieces of their lives logically together to build forward. May our children remember to pick up stones at the most difficult places along their life way, and may we teach them that it is possible to arrange them side by side.

An excellent life is not an unbroken life; an excellent life is a life in which one has intelligently assembled secure stepping stones.

Much love,
Abigail

Velvet Peach

Had I told you about Gwendolyn's fruit baskets?

An excellent life is not one void of sobbing sadness. An excellent life is a life that celebrates through sadness.

> The days through which we struggle, finding no way but never losing the light, will be the most significant we are called to live.
>
> —Robert Collyer

> A small cottage wherein laughter lives is worth more than a castle full of tears.
>
> —Chinese proverb

> Qui ne pleure pas ne voit pas.
>
> —Victor Hugo, Les Miserables

October 24, 2012

Dear Jenya,

My sweet friend, I know you understand jet lag and have felt it each time you flew between Asia and Canada. Your description of "we hit the ground running" rings true. You explained the need to keep going, forcing your body to adjust to the time difference. I feel like that tonight although not jet-lagged. I've been on the go today since six AM.

Clearly, I secret type to you when I can; you are kind, understanding, and patient. I wish you were here. We could clink paper latte cups in an understanding cheer for the mommy taxi run. I often think of my own mom, with her tiny waist, brown bouffant with pin kiss curls on each side. She loved tea-length, bright floral dresses. She was stylish in the *Vogue Magazine* kind of a way. It was the time when big round sunglasses and head scarves tied around the chin were in style. Her handbags were oversized, and she often embarrassed me by rummaging through her bag for the car keys. I've caught myself doing exactly the same, rummaging in the bottom of my too-big purse for my own keys with my daughter standing by, waiting for me.

We do have moments, don't we, when we realize that we are our mother's daughter? We have taken on their mannerisms, phrases, and even their preferences. For me, it is her love of cooking and baking, her bangle bracelets, and the idea of outfits. Even in my daughter, I wonderfully and astonishingly see my mother. Her cheerfulness, her love of baking, her stylish scarves. "Have your outfit ready," she'd say as she would lay various items of mix-and-match clothing out on the bed, deciding which top would match what skirt the best. Her laughter was full and sincere. What astonishes me today, when I remember back, is the fact that she was able to laugh at all.

Gwendolyn, whose pretty, hazel-eyed features became lined with stress, whose eyes sunk with sadness, and whose long delicate fingers wore down, with broken nails and dry-skinned, bleeding cracks along each finger. Gwendolyn, whose diabetic legs refused to heal from open sores and whose eyes went blind. Gwendolyn, whose body filled with fluid and whose broken heart stopped beating.

I felt every moment of my beautiful mother's decline. I watched it unfold before my childhood eyes. I do not know if she really did do what they accused her of. If the thick-necked man who crushed your hand when he shook it and who summertime flirted with my mother's tiny frame did as they said. Truth would not have weighted either way. Once accused, her life was over. I grew up immersed in her pain, filled with her shame, and absorbed in her suffering. Consequences for secrets crashed on my head while my mother lay dying under her pink floral quilt.

I'm unsure if her psychological trauma began before the shunning and was heightened after wards or if most of her mental anguish was as a result of the shunning. I have what my child's mind took in and what my adult mind can figure out. Mommy is sobbing. Mommy is lying on the bed and can't get up. Mommy is angry. Daddy is not here. What if Mommy dies? And yet even in all this, there were times that Mommy Gwendolyn sincerely laughed. "Oh dear," she'd say, "it's from the sublime to the ridiculous." "It's better to laugh than to cry." And so there were times that she chose laughter even in the depths of her ridiculous situation. And, Jenya, it is her laughter that I remember the most on the busy days when she took my tiny four-year-old self with her to the local outdoor Montreal fruit stand. She would choose the best fruit to be assembled in baskets.

We would pile boxes of fresh peaches, apples, pears, bananas, and grapes, both red and green in colour, into our little car. We would sing together as we wound our way home into the kitchen to the round wooden table. My mom would use the fresh fruit to build a beautiful display of sweet, ripe freshness overflowing each basket. She would carefully unroll sheets of clear cellophane to wrap each fruit-filled basket and tie at the top with a trailing ribbon. Each basket would then be loaded into the car, and together, we would drive to the hospitals in downtown Montreal. I remember the peaches being the most delicate but the most delicious of all the fruit piled high. If a peach was accidentally dropped, it would bruise and then not be used in the fruit basket. Instead, it would be saved for cobbler or be sliced up and ladled over vanilla ice cream. I would, my little four-year-old self, help my mother deliver her pretty, freshly made fruit baskets. I remember the weight of the hospital door as I leaned my full body against the door in order to hold it open for my mom. With her arms full, she happily carried the baskets in. The baskets of fruit were sold in the hospital gift stores. It was a creative and lucrative business. Her light yellow business cards read *Panier Du Fruit*. Her laughter and singing as she swirled around, fruit basket in arm, was before the days of shunning. Before she got "fed up" with her marriage and before her family disowned her.

Gwendolyn had married a man of integrity. An intelligent, quiet, caring, and dashing man who, by the time he married her, had suffered much in his young life. My father was one of five boys. Educated and well dressed, he is a man who walks gently through life; a man that holds wise maturity far beyond his peers. My father's mother had died in a Montreal hospital when he was nine years old. Shortly after her death, his father married a strong, no-nonsense, red-headed Irish girl named Janet. Janet took on the responsibility to help this young widower raise his five sons. However, within three years, my father's father, while lying on the bed next to his son, listening to a hockey game, died. My father, beside him on the bed, saw his own father's face turn red, heard his last struggle of breath, could not wake his daddy up, and knew something was terribly wrong. Janet collected her strong and sure-footed self to take on the task as a single stepmother to raise up these five boys in the city of Montreal.

Looking back, my father and mother made a stunning couple. He, mild, well mannered, blue eyed, dark haired, and lean; she, tiny, stylish, enthusiastic, and friendly. Sometimes, Jenya, I look at pictures of them together and see nothing initially wrong. My mother and father, as a young married couple, look picture-perfect. I wonder how things could have gone so amiss and then remember to look below the surface. There is far more to a pretty picture, and there was far more for my mother to cope with in her own self than she could manage. She flew from the two extremes of laughter and business to periods of quiet and low. Her fluctuations were noticeable, and her energy level swings up and swings down were part of our lives. The up days brought laughter; the down days brought crying. Both knit into my memory of my mother. But, Jenya, I choose to remember the sound of my mother's laughter over the sound of her sobbing. The terrible can become beautiful if that is the way you choose to paint it. My mother's tiny waist and tea-length floral dresses, her bouffant kiss-curled hair, her bangle bracelets, and her oversized purses slung over her upturned wrist. Her purse-matching shoes and her scarf ready to tie over her hair. Jenya, my beautiful mother who was suddenly shunned lived a terrible life. A single mother, one who was able to teach her daughter this: "now, dear, it's better to laugh than cry because sometimes, life is from the sublime to the ridiculous."

Oh, Jenya, divorce can spiral down into the depths of ridiculous cruelty. It can become so horrible that one spouse takes all the household belongings and, at the same time, gets full custody of the children.

As in my childhood, my sister and I did not see my father for seven years. However, seven long years later, after imagining what that man might look like and wishing him back over and over, my sister went into the city to find our father. She found an insightful, patient, kind, and loving man; a man who had waited for his daughters. The first time I saw my daddy, after that seven-year gap, he stood straight in his navy blue gold-buttoned, double-breasted blazer, white shirt, and perfectly-knotted tie. He took his two daughters out for dinner. I was a very young girl, nervous of this man I did not know. While sitting at the restaurant table meeting him, I choked on my very first sip of water. He calmly handed my embarrassed self his white freshly ironed handkerchief. I used it to cover my water-sputtering mouth, grateful for this unfamiliar man's extended gentleness.

Aime Wren

Our father spent years gently recovering and restoring the relationship that he had lost with his daughters. Healing flowed in torrents, and I now type not only knowing my father but loving him dearly, esteeming him highly, and seeking to honor him always.

There are days when the memory of my mother's laughter keeps me going. When you have heard both, Jenya, make sure to remember the sounds of laughter more than the sounds of sobbing. I remember that even when the bruised peach wasn't useful to be displayed and sold in the basket, it was not thrown out. It was cut up, its fresh, wet peach juice dripping out healthy fruit goodness and deliciously served over ice cream. The bruised peaches were not thrown out.

My mother's sobs flooded her whole body; she shook in expressed agony. As I lay next to her in the bed, I curled up, my knees tucked in tightly to my chest, my arms wrapped around them. I hear the sounds of her crying and remember the hard knot in my then eight-year-old stomach. Jenya, my mommy sobbed because the shunning was so severe, but it is her laughter I choose to remember.

An excellent life is not one void of sobbing sadness; an excellent life is a life that celebrates through sadness.

Much love,
Abigail

Robin's Egg Aqua

Had I told you about my field treasure finds?

An excellent life is not a life that ignores death. An excellent life is one that finds strength in the struggle to live.

To strive, to seek, to find, and not to yield.
—Alfred Lord Tennyson

All nature is but Art, unknown to thee;
All chance, direction which thou canst not see.

—Alexander Pope, "An Essay on Man"

There is a kind of release that comes directly to those who have undergone an ordeal and who know, having survived it, that they are equal to all of life's occasions.

—Lewis Mumford

October 21, 2012

Dear Jenya,

Last week, the sky was spectacular both at the beginning and at the end of the day. It is not every day that I get to see this. At the beginning, I drove my thirteen-year-old son to his school volleyball tryouts. At the end of the same day, I was again in the car, driving my same son to his community hockey game. We saw the sunrise and the sunset together. This precious time with my boy looking at the spectacular awe-inspiring glowing display in the sky at the beginning and the end of the day. Because we were driving, we saw both in passing. I cannot help but hold the sight in my mind and relive the feeling. The beginning and the end of a day while passing through with my son. I pointed out the obviously red, glowing-day-beginning beauty. I mentioned to him, "George, there will be times in your life when you doubt if a sovereign hand exists. When you doubt, make sure to look at the sunrise or the sunset. That, son, will remind you, and you will know why I have assurance." My boy nodded that cool teenage acknowledgment, as if saying, "I get you, Mom."

And he does. This smart, thoughtful, now-tall lanky boy understands me. His appreciation of the live theater production *War Horse*, his taste for foreign food, his willingness to listen, his kindness to young children, his nature and appearance—exactly like my father's. This boy understands the significance of the beginning and the end with the sunrise and sunset, and he felt the connection of sharing together the fragile gift of life that we have been given for one more exceptional day. This sunset moment that gave me another reminder brimming with assurance of the frame for our lives. The beginning of a new day and the close of that day copies the pattern of the emerging of a season and the finish of that season. The unfolding of life and the closing of that life is the same pattern. The cycle-regeneration life pattern repeats itself. Jenya, I see the renewal design as unmistakable, a design painted in power in the sky more than once in a day over the entire world for all people of all nations to see. It is a sovereign, universal painting, every morning and every night, offered for every human being to admire.

The sovereign puts a beginning and a close to each day, sets seasons, renewing, refreshing and resting the earth and made the earth to accept our bodies when we are memorialized in death.

I buried my mother in the month of August, and as the trees in Canada began to turn colours that fall, I wondered for the first time why summer death, called autumn, is so beautiful. The end-of-summer death transition to winter is, in Canada, wildly colourful. Every tree screams vibrant displays of red, yellow, orange, and burgundy, making a Canadian autumn very gorgeous. Winter blows in cold, snowy, icy, and silent. Death falls over the earth for a season, the pearl white blanket of snow lays as a peaceful blanket of comfort over the hills and valleys, over the farmers' fields, and on city landscapes. Each individually designed delicate snowflake is a masterpiece of intricate workmanship. A frozen beauty that becomes a blanket, covering everything in winter sleep. Animals hibernate, snow insulates, pond life is on hold, and the lakes freeze over. All creation sleeps, waiting for the spring sunshine to awaken it. Each year, the warmth of sunshine beams melts the snow, awakens the animals, calls back the birds, and pushes the sap.

Death is sleeping until spring. I saw this the very first spring after that August, the August in which I laid my mother in the ground. I looked at the fresh green bud peeking its way out of the soil, I felt the warm sunshine melting the dark frozen earth, and I could feel her alive, awake on the other side. We had done everything medically possible, but we knew that diabetes and congestive heart failure would take her.

Jenya, after four years of exhausted running, tending, palliative care agonizing, and blind struggle suffering, my sister and I held hands and together stood beside our father and buried our mother. Our beautiful mother whose life had never recovered. Who lay blind in her hospital and nursing home bed, her legs swollen and numb. Her feet hard and cold to the touch, her face puffy, and her lips pale and, on bad days, blue. Gwendolyn, who chatted cheerily with her nurses, who listened to George Beverly Shea sing "The Old Rugged Cross" on the round white CD player on her bedside table. Gwendolyn, whose death-hovering stays in cardiac care ICU were long and many, who knew what it was to be intubated and extubated, who depended on Lasix, oxygen, and Prednisone. Gwendolyn, who let her youngest daughter administer injections of insulin, turn up her oxygen, and agreed not to bother the overworked nurses for something as simple as a fresh facecloth or towel but that I should quietly find the door labeled Linen Closet and get what we needed. I learned that a hospital room right next to the nurses station is louder and busier in the hallway but a better luck of the draw because your loved one is checked on more often than if she's at the far end of the hallway. Doctors do rounds at certain times, and if you miss their five-minute stop by, you could have missed crucial cardiac information for a solid week. I learned that some death comes in warning waves. It is like an ocean current pulling heartbeats excruciatingly low and then a drug-forced, machine-enhanced rally back up. These death waves were spread over months, blanketing my heart in hospital running stress and constant fear. Struggling to hold moments, to pull precious time with both my arms toward us, to appreciate beauty in a potted hospital windowsill plant.

Then on that day, four years and much sickness later, her lips were blue, the back of her neck still warm, and her body was stiff. She did not respond to my voice; she didn't move at my tears. I bent over top of my mother, resting my head on her chest, alone in her nursing home room as George Beverly Shea played for one last time. It was my turn to shake in uncontrollable agony, the same shaking expression of pain that she had felt in her bed those agonizing years before when I, as a child, had slept next to her at night. The sadness exhaustion and brutality of our untold suffering spilled out and filled that little nursing home room. Puddles of tear-flowing pity grew deep. On that day, I had no boots to splash in any puddle; I just sank into the watery well of sadness. The light pink walls watched in silence as they took her body away. Her nurses, kind and compassionate, had been trained for this very moment and spoke through my daze. Gwendolyn's nurses gave me simple practical instructions as to what to do next. I did exactly what they told me to do. I had no idea otherwise.

I knelt down and packed my mother's belongings, the things that had been reduced in necessity to one small room. Her bangle bracelets, her stylish but comfortable sweaters, her creams and powders, and her slip-on shoes. I folded her floral quilt and gathered up nursing home meal menus. By myself, I gently set my mother's things into odd-sized boxes, loaded them into the trunk of my car, and drove in a ten-minute, off-city road from her nursing home to my own home. For one night, I slumbered in exhausted shock and drove for four hours the next day to meet my sister and my mother's transported body in the village of shunning.

Her funeral was held in the town, and she was buried on the village hill. Gwendolyn's grave was dug in the dark August earth in front of Gladys's. The memory of the weight of carrying my mother's peach silk lined coffin is still in my arms. The smell of the hospital hallways, the sound of the life support machines, those dear people we befriended who died before my mother did are vivid, aching memories of reality. At the time, the pink walls watched me cry over her dead blue lips. She was sixty-six, and I was thirty-three years old.

I stood in the small town, in the tiny wooden-pewed, stain glass-windowed chapel and read the memorial poem I had written for her. I could only stand that day beside my mother's coffin with enough courage to speak because, as a child, I had learned about robin's egg aqua from my field treasure finds.

My Momma

"Abigail!" you did say, when you were cross
Sit up straight, look like a lady
No elbows on the table
And always be able.
Speak politely—respect your elders
Don' talk back,
Mind your manners . . .

Yes, my momma . . . I would comply
As you were training me for what would lie
Ahead . . .
Those years went on
And I did see
Why you did intend
Those commands to be

As now I,
A momma too . . .
I repeat the same
To my own three . . . just a training time
For little saplings—to forge roots, to grow up,
Strong and tall,
Straight and sure . . .

You did the training well, my momma
All, all on your own
You worked and cared,
You worked and cried
Often out loud, you questioned, "Why?"

Yes, manners remembered
Character made
Mom, with cheerfulness flowing
And compassion displayed
You extended forgiveness
Always anchored in hope
You soldiered on
Daily forced to be strong.

Fruit baskets, catering platters, a bakery or two
Children by the many, you did lovingly tend
Always a helping hand you willingly did lend
Garage sales you didn't want to miss
Ink circles marked the paper
With happy chatter on your lips
You and your daughter did caper

Straw-lined fields on summer days
Our baskets laden full
Fresh berries, in hot sunshine we did weigh
Full days, of happy memories all along the way

I do not question
I know you lived with good intention
You made the best of every situation
You cracked jokes, and you found fun
Laughter amidst depletion

Until one day
I stood by your side
And little Abigail May
Became your guide
My hand on yours to lead
My eyes for you, you could not see
My arm for you to steady be
My voice when you could not speak
I gave my all for you, my momma
Because you gave your all for me
No moment of care would I begrudge
You gave your life to raise and love
Two little girls,
And I,
I, the last

So today I do cast
A flower on your grave
Momma, I honor you today
Knowing that your suffering time
Has passed

In heaven,
You now have—
Hands that do not shake,
Take Grandma's hands in yours
Eyes that can see

Gaze at the sparkling, crystal river.
Steady legs
You have to walk on bridges of transparent gold
Your voice is clear,
Clear to speak and sing,
Hallelujahs to the Almighty King
Momma, may you feel strength that never fades
As you watch us from above
May you have a heavenly joy indwelling
A fullness that allows no room for sadness
No sorrow, no regret
A full, deep, perfect joy
Accept today, this joy complete
As you have left a deep imprint

Yes, manners remembered
Character made
Mom, with cheerfulness flowing
And compassion displayed
You offered forgiveness
You chose to be an open witness

And as you hear me speak,
May you, my momma
Think with pride today
"That girl, that one . . . the youngest
She is my Abigail May"
And may you know
How privileged I am
To honor you today,
Who has just died
You, you were
My momma.

Four days after we buried her body, I woke up at my cottage, lingering in the sleepy fog of nauseated disbelief that death had come, my mind unable to process the truth of her loss while at the same time a fearful, flooding realization that my in-law family had not cancelled or delayed their vacation plans. I crawled out of my soft robin's eggs blue sheet-covered bed, collected myself together, prepared the cottage, and welcomed all thirty-one of them. I made their meals, gave those who stayed overnight fresh beds to sleep in, and hostess chatted. How I was physically able to do this, I have little comprehension of. The earth had not settled on my mother's grave. I was utterly reeling from her loss, but the clear expectation existed that I would continue to function happily and fulfill my role. In a few stolen moments, just before serving one of the large meals, I had everything baked and tossed, simmered, and stirred. The table was set, and I floated amidst brothers—and sisters-in-law, nieces, and nephews. As I stepped into the walk-in closet, I saw an almost-empty bottle of amber liquid. It sat golden, glowing at me on the ledge of the shelf. Charles had left the bottle there from the previous weekend men's visit. Unfamiliar to me, I had asked the men what kind of glass to serve such strong amber in and had boated across the bay to get ice to place under it. Jenya, with all my in-laws at my cottage, my mother's grave dug earth still unsettled, with forcefully restrained grief threatening to flood over in torrents, I hid in the pantry, opened the bottle, and felt the deep burn of the liquid all the way down the inside of my aching chest. One spicy shocking sip was enough. I recapped that bottle, used both my hands to flatten the wrinkles in my soft red sundress, stood up tall, and smiled my way out of that pantry. I had guests to serve dinner to. Of course they wouldn't have delayed their holiday. In those, with Brethren-thinking minds, my mother had been already dead for years.

Jenya I stood then calmed by the sip of amber, and secretly reminded myself of the robins eggs. As a child playing in the spring fields on the far side of the laneway over the hill, I found many field treasures. The very best treasure was to find a robin's egg. Sometimes whole and intact, the egg would have fallen from the nest. Other times, the shell was cracked, showing the place where the baby bird had hatched out.

This find would delight my little girl mind. I would stare at its fragile eggshell beauty and marvel at its tiny brown speckles. Sometimes, the shell would be a clear, smooth, bright robin's egg blue, speckle-free. This life shell, cracked to set the bird free, is again the cycle-proof picture. The bird grows inside the shell until strong enough to crack its way out. It is true that you can't help a baby bird hatch. Part of its strengthening process is to set itself free from the shell. If you break the shell to help the baby bird hatch, the well-intentioned helping becomes a hindrance. The fragile baby bird has strength enough to hatch out of its shell and then strength and skill enough to fly. Soon, its bright red breast will grace the sky, hop along the porch, and feed from seed at the feeder. Robin's egg blue hatching showed my child's mind the marvelous fragility of life hatched into the strength of flight. Our struggle for life and our struggle for flight is a necessary strengthening.

So, Jenya, as the sunrise signals the beginning of a new day, I remember beautifully speckled, cracked robins' eggs from my childhood field treasure finds. As a tiny girl, I saw truth in a robin's egg, I saw power painted in a sunset, and I saw purity in a raindrop.

To me nature was the only thing that expressed the existence of a sovereign hand with no hypocrisy. I figured that my mother's palliative care days were the struggle to break free of her shell and fly . . . the way I see it, dying is cracking the egg shell from the inside out.

An excellent life is not a life that ignores death; an excellent life is one that finds strength in the struggle to live.

Much love,
Abigail

Had I told you about the killdeer plover's nest, my navy blue shoes, the red dress, and Grandma's violets? Had I told you about my stepping-stones, the piled-up peaches, and the tiny robin's eggshells?

Dear Jenya, had I told you that an excellent life is like an excellent painting?

An excellent life designs its own nest of safety; it is a life lived in compassion despite cruelty. An excellent life holds ironclad hope under humiliation, and it blooms in the beauty of reality. An excellent life is not one that is unbroken. It is a life that has intelligently arranged stepping-stones, finding strength in the struggle to live.

An excellent life is able to celebrate through sadness all while purposefully composing a painting of deep dimension, beautiful balance, and vibrant colour. A life hand painted from which music can be heard.

> My father-in-law hired artisans to come to Tongkou and paint additional friezes under our eves . . . everything is painted . . . exactly as it happened.
>
> —Lisa See, Snow Flower and the Secret Fan

> Faded away like the stars in the morning,
> Losing their light in the glorious sun—
> Thus would we pass from this earth and it's toiling,
> Only remembered for what we have done.

Shall we be missed though by others succeeded,
Reaping the fields we in spring time have sown?
No, for the sower may pass from their labors,
Only remembered for what they have done.

Only the truth in the life we have spoken
Only the seed that in life we have sown
These shall pass onwards when we are forgotten
Only remembered for what we have done.

Who'll sing the anthem and who'll tell the story
Will the line hold will it scatter and run
Shall we at last be united in glory
Only remember for what we have done.

> *—musical score for War Horse,*
> *words by Horatius Bonar,*
> *music by Ira D. Sankey,*
> *arranged by John Tams and H. Brough*

An excellent painting is designed with three main components. It has deep dimension, it displays beautiful balance, and it is vibrant in colour. An excellent painting is heard and remembered.

Jenya, had I mentioned dimension, beautiful balance, and vibrant colour? Had I talked about highlights, clear varnish, and restoration? Had I chatted to you about opposition, welcome variety, and custom-made frames? These are the lessons learned in my yellow-walled, red-sofa-placed painting studio.

Deep Dimension

The dimension is created by beginning with placing dark paint onto the prepared canvas. If the artist fails to place the dark paint first, an oil painting will lack dimension. It is much harder, if not impossible, to get the same deep dimension of the image by putting dark oil paint on top of the light. The paint mixes together on the canvas, blending, leaving little or no contrast with no definition. And so it is with life; dark days of suffering may come first, but when they do, one must know that light days of celebration come after. It is our dark days of suffering with our light days of celebration touched over the top that paints deep dimension into each of our lives. Dark days of tragedy, suffering, and crisis actually sculpt and shape the image. The darkness of suffering shapes a deep dimension of a person that could otherwise not be achieved. The dark days are necessary, and when light days of celebration are placed on top, a shape is gained that could otherwise not be formed. This contrast between dark and light is, in drawing and painting, an ancient technique called chiaroscuro. It is the dimension design of chiaroscuro in our lives that is the excellence. Jenya, I was the little girl who sat alone at the back of the meeting, brutalized by a culture that forbade music, dancing, alcohol, makeup, stylish clothes, and friendships with people outside of the group. However, the fair-haired child grew up, and years later, you could find her at her very first birthday party, surrounded by trustworthy, intelligent friends. We celebrated with music playing; we sipped glasses of chilled white wine. We outlined our lips with cheerful coloured gloss, we wore stylish dresses, and we danced.

Beautiful Balance

An excellent painting offers beautiful balance, no matter what kind
of a painting—impressionistic, realistic, abstract, ancient, or modern.
Those admiring the work will immediately look for balance. Like an
admired painting, an excellent life needs to be well-balanced. Time
balanced into an organized day, a well-planned month in a logical
calendar year. Health is considered by a balance in diet, the continual
balance of rest and activity. A mind balanced in perspective, in
well-formulated opinions, and steadfast decision making. An intellect
balanced in the study of history and an update of current events. A
balanced academic appreciation of science and respect for the arts.
A heart emotionally balanced with mercy, kindness, and compassion
on one side of the scale with justice, rule of democratic law, and
consequence on the other. Balance is a continual effort and not easy
to achieve. I test my balance each summer morning while out in my
rowing scull, knowing that one prideful moment, one slip of the hand,
one disrespect of the sport and I could get wet, tipped fully into the
lake in a moment.

Balance is painted one brushstroke and lived one day at a time. It
begins with each well-balanced individual, bringing balance to their
home, stability to their community, and good leadership in their
nation. An excellent life is like an excellent painting. It is perfectly and
beautifully well-balanced.

Vibrant Colour

An excellent painting is vibrant in shades of colour. Colour jumps out
as either pleasing or unpleasing, as vibrant or boring. In a painting,
so as in life, colour, Jenya, is universal. It was the first thing I tested
the little children on and then taught them in the small bay windowed
kindergarten classroom. My students, at four years old, learned their
colours. This simplicity is a serious secret to a successful painting and
a successful life. When things get very complex, when troubles are

too big and far beyond our control—my answer is to simplify. Learn my colours, live my own day very well, simply and graciously paint my own painting. Simplify down to the very basics of kindergarten; learn and choose your colours for your painting, and likewise learn and choose your character for life. Character colours show in the decisions that we make each day. Anthony Hopkins showed the colours of the character he played, Charles Morse, in the movie *The Edge*. "Most people lost in the wilderness die of shame. They didn't do the one thing that could save their lives—thinking," says Charles to his rival. Likewise, Jean Valjean was an exceptional example of daily integrity in the choices that he makes throughout the classic tale set in France, *Les Miserables*. It is our daily choices that are the colour mixing of our painting. The kindness spoken, the stranger reached out to, the child comforted, the spouse encouraged, duty done, integrity maintained.

Jenya, I want to mix my shades of character and paint in love, not hate; good, not evil; colour that stands for the preservation of life, not death. Shades that respect others, not that devise annihilation of them. Character of colour that champions freedom, not dictatorship. I want the colour of truth and honesty painted in triumph over lies and deceit. The colour, Jenya, of kindness never means spiritedness of human value, not human humiliation. Let us paint the colour of protection for our children, not the enslavement of them. The colours of faith, not fundamental extremism. Just as colour is so evident in a painting, so character is evident in a person's life.

I know that the mix of shades and tones of colour are limitless. There are numerous blends and recipes of mixes. Beautifully thick oil paint blended on the palette with the palette knife, producing many gorgeous options of colour. The variety one can mix is new each day; it is rejuvenating, exciting, and thrilling to see a new, fresh shade of pink come to life on a palette. The rose colour that I will dab on the cheeks of the child's portrait is fresh and new each time I mix and match it. As colour of character differs and personality offers us wonderful variety, we each differ, but within our differences, individual character matters.

Jenya, the underlying principles for drawing and painting exist. They are the fundamentals. Classic principles are taught in fundamental drawing and painting classes, giving a solid intellectual structure from which one's own creativity is launched through and off of. From what I have learned, the construction drawing is crucial to any painting; it is the architectural undergirding on which the work will be built. And so in life, there is a framework on which to build. A logical, well-planned, thoughtfully placed, insightfully designed construction drawing on which our very own colour-mixed character is placed. Can one achieve a painting without knowing the fundamentals and without acknowledging the existence of the academic architectural drawing? Yes. But I would argue that acknowledging the classic principles and applying these general rules is a foundation that I want my own free creativity to be built on. Likewise, I want my life painting to have a solid construction drawing. And that is why I consider a sovereign hand. That a supreme power would draw my life and that I, in turn, would paint well over this design for me.

As I stand and admire the work of Monet or marvel at Michelangelo's masterpieces, I wait and listen at each painting for a song. In some cases, the song comes immediately—it may be a celestial praise, a loud concerto, a deep drumbeat, or a child's musical rhyme. I have admired an excellent painting of brilliantly placed poppies and imagined music. Jenya, it was as if the poppies painted on the canvas were swaying to music playing in the wind. Have you ever stood and admired a painting and heard a song in your mind playing from it? Have you heard Robert Starer's *Sketches in Colour: Seven Pieces for Piano* played in concert? Starer has put colours to music.

Oh, that it could be this way with my life painting—that when others look at it, they hear the most excellent, the most beautiful music. Jenya, a sovereign hand draws the construction of each of our lives, one that gives each of us talents in which to paint, and as we work daily to paint well, music is written. Imagine the music of each of our lives being played together in concert!

Jenya, the music played from a life painting has power. Remember Sarajevo? The melodic, triumphant music of the cello played for twenty-two days on the street of Sarajevo in the middle of the war. In Steven Galloway's novel, for those brief moments, the cellist's music calmed the sniper, stopped the bullets, and brought beauty in the midst of destruction and ruin.

The cellist opens his eyes. The sadness she saw in his face is gone. She doesn't know where it went. His arms rise, and his left hand grips the neck of the cello, his right guides the bow to its throat. It is the most beautiful thing she has ever seen. When the first notes sound they are, to her, inaudible. Sound has vanished from the world. She leans back into the wall. She's no longer there. Her mother is lifting her up, spinning her around and laughing. (Steven Galloway, *The Cellist of Sarajevo*, page 62)

Jenya, music has power, power enough to pause a sniper.

Highlights

In an oil painting, the construction drawing is laid first, dark strokes are then placed, and finally, light shades are then delicately, decidedly, and crucially placed on top. The final touch that artist's brush dabs on, the completing touches, are called the highlights. In oil painting, they cannot be placed ahead of the rest; if so, adding the darks will be very difficult, if not impossible, and dimension will be lost. So the last touches, the highlights, are the most exciting for the artist to place. They are touches of shining beauty placed after hours of hard work. Highlights are final, quick, well-placed splashes that catch the light. In order to mix paint that is useful for highlights, one must use white. White, Jenya, is called the mixing colour. It is what is used to mix into all the other colours to lighten them. Adding variations of white, or simply white itself, changes each colour, allowing for tints, tones, and shades. White, the colour of peace, the colour of the celestial realm, is our painted reference to peace. This white, when mixed into the other colours, lightens them. Just as peace when embedded in individuals and when embraced by nations is our highlight goal. We want to live each day with a sense of calm and peace in our individual lives and in our communities.

A painting is not finished until it's been touched with highlights, just as humanity is not fully achieved until it is established in peace. As in life, our final years are the highlight years. When our hair is graying, when our months are numbered by a physician's diagnosis, when we know that we are painting our final twenty years or our final twenty days, we have the ability to touch the canvas of our lives with the most important—the crucial well-placed highlights. We can catch the light and place it on our life painting. We can complete our painting with the best part, the final touch that makes our painting perfect. Jenya, in our lives we find a pure spiritual white; we can mix the spiritual in with each colour, giving our days and our painting life. It is this spiritual light, this peaceful pearl-mixing white, in whatever way we acknowledge or recognize it, shining through and within our painting, that allow the brushstrokes on our canvas to become a shining of the divine. Highlights placed on a canvas are glorious. They make the painting sing. They offer a lasting song, one heard long after the painting is framed.

Jenya my friend, it is the last note the choir sings, the grand finale, the encore at the concert, that is the climax highlight of the music. And then our physical life is framed, but our canvas is appreciated and music is heard from it long after our death.

Signature

Have you found yourself admiring a painting and then stepping closer in order to look for the artist's signature? We look for a full name, initials, stamp, or identifying mark. As children, we are taught in school to place our name on our schoolwork. Simply so that the teacher can identify what belongs to us and can evaluate each student's work. We write our given names on our papers, claiming responsibility—perhaps shyly, maybe proudly—for what we are submitting. When the artist places their name on their work, they are doing the same thing. A name placed not only claims the work as one's own but takes responsibility for it. We declare, "This is what I have done." In fear or in failure, in assurance or in alarm, in pain or in pleasure—this is what I have painted. Will others understand the painting? We ask ourselves. Will they admire, dismiss, or dismantle the work? Will it be lasting? We ask ourselves, will what I do in my life be lasting? When I sign my life painting, I take responsibility for it. This is my life, and this is what I have done. "Recte faciendo neminem timeas." By doing good, you shall fear no one.

Clear Varnish

Once dry, often the artist will apply a kind of varnish or sealant to the painting. This clear coat covers the oil paint as a protective layer, but it also draws out the colour.

Varnish makes the colours more vibrant, just as rainwater when it touches the earth makes the colours of the field brighter. Like the surface of the water, when one looks below the surface, they see more clearly. When the artist varnishes their painting, Jenya, the colours shine brighter under this wet protective coat. Varnish allows the colour to shine more brightly beneath the surface. Just as you and I know, to always, always look below the surface. And to allow that clear, wet liquid to do its job. It is intended to protect and to make the colours shine brighter.

Restoration

In my studio, I have had the breathtaking pleasure of restoring 150-year-old paintings originally painted by my relative in Montreal under the teaching direction of Krieghoff. His paintings have survived for six generations. Each of these two made their way to me. One traveled from a garage through an estate auction. It spent years resting in the back of a child's closet and finally was handed to me in a derelict-looking bag by my sister.

The other was a gift from a kind and intelligent relative who appreciated that I had restored one of his paintings. He sent the small treasure neatly wrapped in brown paper with a thank-you note addressed to me. My studio walls now hold both heirlooms that I have cleaned, touched up, and restored. Their new vintage-style frames made me thrill almost as much as when my tiny brush first touched the same canvas that my relative had painted 150 years ago.

The man is gone, but his paintings hang on my light yellow wall. They speak of who he was and who influenced his colours. They hold the story of his life for my children to learn about. Jenya, a man will die, but his painting lives on. The music from it can be heard for generations. It is as though the kindness of one person has the power to restore another, even 150 years later. My brush touched up the painting originally done by this man six generations earlier. We don't live unto ourselves; our lives touch others.

Internal and External Opposition

As we paint, we must count on and prepare for opposition. There are many factors that oppose, prevent, and pressure us. Some paintings are defaced, some are disregarded, many are mocked, and others are misunderstood. All artists have faced both external and internal opposition. We know the struggle to find time, to fight through creative blocks, to develop a style all our own, or to learn a new technique. It is no easy task to get that finished product to appear even close to what we have in mind. And even then, when our internal doubt and struggle for self-confidence is surmounted, we may well face external comments from others laced with disdain. "All you do is paint pictures . . ." It takes years of effort, a lifetime of lessons, and serious self-motivation to continue to work in a surpassing strength that overcomes all opposition.

Prepare for opposition in life, both external and internal, and use it as your driving force to become even more resolutely skilled at what you do. Because as each painting requires determined, unrelenting, positive perseverance toward the finishing touches, so each of our lives, Jenya, requires the same. Determined, unrelenting, ironclad, hope-filled, positive perseverance toward the goal of completion. It is gentle determination mixed with silent hope that propels me to open my slim silver Apple and secretly type to you. I recognize the opposition, but my friend, I'm continuing to paint one tiny unnoticed keystroke at a time.

Welcome Variety

Let us use the right tools, determine the texture, develop the contours, and refine our skills along the way. May we choose the colours of our lives for our own painting, in recognition of a sovereign who paints the sky for all to see, reminding us that there is a beginning and an end. There is a start to each painting and a completion of it. Some take minutes to finish, others take years. Excellence is not in the amount of time taken to paint; rather, it is deeply embedded in the work itself. Excellence is not measured in years, for the brush does not know the age of the hand that holds it. Excellence is found inside the painting; it is measured in the deep dimension, beautiful balance, and vibrant colour.

Jenya, excellent paintings hang in museums around the world. They hang in small studios, out-of-the-way cafes; they are propped up in hovels, and they are pinned proudly on school bulletin boards. Some are accidentally crumpled in children's backpacks, others painted on church ceilings, in henna ink on women's hands; others are etched on the walls of ancient hidden caves. Excellent paintings are carved and coloured; they are layered and restored. Some are displayed and others are hidden. They are found in mountaintop lodges, seaside beach houses, and in gated castles. Excellent paintings are auctioned for millions or disregarded in garage sales. Some canvases have been craftily stolen by thieves while others are made by tiny hands and shyly handed to Grandma. Excellent paintings curve gracefully around calligraphy and sit neatly illustrating ancient literature. Excellent paintings are inked on ladies' hands; they are marked on glass, carved and coloured into wood, embellished on seashells, set on stones, and heated into fabric.

The variety is limitless, and the excellence is astounding. In every country around the world, the beauty of painted humanity is endless.

Custom-Made Frame

Like paintings, when completed, each of our lives will one day be custom framed.

The frame is the crown of the work. It is a complimentary completion that matches perfectly. The frame adds weight to the canvas and is the setting for it.

There are many choices and kinds of frames, and it takes a knowledgeable, discerning eye to properly match the work with the frame. When it is matched well, it compliments the work, secures the work, and allows it to be well displayed. A custom-made frame completes the artwork. In the same final completion, with the intelligent design of the original construction drawing, the sovereign artist will frame our lives, and the master composer will write music that flows from the painting.

Much love,
Abigail

The Lord appeared to us in the past, saying: I have loved you with an everlasting love; I have drawn you with unfailing kindness.

—Jeremiah 31:3, NIV

A sovereign hand draws the layout, the placement, and the chiaroscuro construction drawing for each of our lives. We then pick up our life brush and paint over the drawing in shades, hues, tones, and choices of vibrant colour. We allow the divine to shine light while mixing our personal colours and placing our crucial highlights. After which time, an amount of time that we do not know, a sovereign hand presents an individual custom-made frame for each of our hand-painted lives. The frame has been specially designed for our life painting. It is perfectly suited to the painting that we have been working on. And as the frame is being built, as we have been working hard at our brushstrokes, music is being composed to match. Musical notes strung together in harmony of individuals' lives. Music that is then one day played in unison—a choir of all people from all nations. Jenya, are there paintings hung in a heavenly gallery with music sung and played in celestial orchestras, bands, and choirs, a culmination of lives lived well? Are there millions of paintings hung on marble walls, in a heavenly gallery? Each of our lives on celestial display?

Because an excellent life is like an excellent painting, and one can hear music playing from each life, so then we stand together in admiration of what individuals have accomplished with the chiaroscuro drawing that they have been given.

If we knew each other's secrets, what comfort we would find.

—John Churton Collins

Later, the police asked me, why I had risked my life fighting for a bag. Trembling and in pain, I explained, "It had my book in it." "A book?" a policeman exclaimed. "Is a book more important than your life?" In so many ways, my book was my life.

—Xinran, prologue of *The Good Women of China: Hidden Voices*

November 1, 2012

Dear Jenya,

Had I told you about my seven colours, Jenya? Had I painted you this picture sooner, would you not have hung yourself.

Had you told me that you were suffering, struggling in your mind, could I have been the friend and help that you needed to choose life? You mentioned your sister, our long over-lunch discussion about the struggle of depression echoes in my head. You did tell me that your sister suffered, but you did not tell me you felt the same. I admired your well-mannered, polite, trustworthy discretion. I do know the pressure to paint the picket fence white. When things are not good, we get out our cans of white exterior. We put a fresh coat on that picket fence, pretending, smiling, holding it all together for our children, for family name, reputation, and social appearances. I now see how dangerous whitewashing is. Jenya, you repainted your white picket fence and died while doing so.

They say one gets to a point with this kind of illness when you can't even call out for help. Somewhere in your mind, you got lost. So lost that you found what you needed in your closet and hung yourself in the shower. You chose what to use. You figured out how to tie the right kind of knot. Had you tested the distance from the highest shower bar to the tile floor? How many mornings did you stand in that very same place with the warm water raining down over your naked body? How many mornings did the warm water comfort you until its wet dripping lost all and any ability to soothe your pain and your mind then decided? Your hand wrote your very last letter, . . . you turned your face up towards the shower water, and all your life colour washed away.

My tall, smart, beautiful, educated, well-traveled, married mother of two. My international e-mail pen pal, summer cottage neighbor. Looking back, I had only one sign in the snapshot pictures of your family. The pictures taken when you were not looking at the camera; you looked terribly sad. I noticed the serious sadness in your face, but it did not match with the life you described. Your empty, black circle-rimmed eyes were not the eyes of the friend who boated over to my dock, the girl who shared a salad with me, the girl who sat outside with me one whole afternoon for tea. I wish I had opened the gate to my white picket fence and let you in closer.

Medication did not work, counseling did not reach you, and your body grew lifeless at the harm of your own hand. I can't comprehend this illness that takes a smart mind—the life of a young woman. I would have screamed no. I would have begged you pleading. I would have visited you in the hospital and prayed for your recovery. Instead, here I sit with this secret, typing to you from Starbucks, wiping tears from my blurry eyes with the sleeve of my sweater. Learning for the first time that statistics report over one million people commit suicide each year.

As it turns out, water can refresh a girl, or it can drown her. Letters can uplift a life or take one. But friendship, true friendship, is simply shown by how we help each other paint. "Water is the driving force of all nature," wrote Leonardo da Vinci.

I needed sovereign-given girlhood resilience to stand in the rain, and it required forced insight to find the colours and see below the surface. It was then, my dear friend, that the terrible became beautiful. Because that is the way I choose to paint it.

Seven colours. Seven colours of an insignificant girl's life not typed in time.

Much love,
Abigail

Abigail's Memorial to Jenya

*A friend is a person with whom I may be
sincere, before him I may think aloud.*

—Ralph Waldo Emerson

*Now you belong to heaven and the stars
spell out your name.*

—Elton John

The Lady

Jenya displayed sophistication, intelligence, and grace. She was sophisticated—in style, class, and travel. Intelligent in conversation, well-read in literature, and gifted in organization. Jenya was graceful in attitude, laughter, and poise. Our sophisticated, intelligent, graceful lady has, by her life in various ways and on various continents, written a letter in each of our hearts.

Her Letter

Jenya—as a daughter, sister, friend, colleague, wife, and mother—has penned a letter in each of us. With each happy memory shared, every cultural trip taken, every Christmas celebrated, birthday prepared for, spa treatment looked forward to, high tea sipped, walk with her dogs taken, for every cottage boat ride, luncheon lingered over, swim meet attended, foundation project begun . . . her letter was deeply inscribed in each of us. Jenya's beauty is inked in permanence; her calligraphy in our lives is lovely.

Our Legacy

Lay down all blame. May we not blame ourselves or blame others. Live beyond these tragic days by arming ourselves against confusion. May her family, friends, and loved ones honor Jenya by becoming people who, from this, grow strong in character. Let us stand together in tragedy and live lives that outshine this shadow of silencing sorrow.

Pearl White:
the Mixing Colour of Peace

"One of these centuries," said Danneskjold, "the brutes, private or public, who believe that they can rule their betters by force, will learn the lesson of what happens when brute force encounters mind and force."

—Ayn Rand, Atlas Shrugged

There can be no keener revelation of a society's soul than the way it treats its children.

—Nelson Mandela

Peace cannot be achieved through violence; it can only be attained through understanding.

—Ralph Waldo Emerson

The secret to an excellent painting and an excellent life is found not only in the colours but in the pearl. White paint is used to make all the other colours lighter and is the colour of the white flag, the pearl of surrender, and peace. Pearl white, peace, mixed in the character and colour of our lives, is light for each individual as we paint our days. No matter what nationality we have been born as or what country we may live in, as humans, we generally desire to find individual purpose to living now and peace in what comes after this life. Purpose and peace are human desires that unite all of us in the painting of humanity. May there be peace established for the purpose of protecting the children of every nation. The solution to the international painting of peace may very well lie in the recognition of the inherent value the lives of all of our nations children. When humanity elevates every child worldwide to the place they deserve, the place of being precious, we will no longer have a mind to harm ourselves or to harm each other. We will, in all nations and all communities and under all circumstances, value life as precious. Precious enough to help each other paint and precious enough to paint in pearl white lives of peacefulness. We will together paint a painting of freedom, respect, education, and peace for the next generation.

As we continue to look below the surface of the water of our lives, we can find our coping colours. When we allow the water of life's circumstances to refresh us, it is deep below the surface that we find the pearl. The white pearl of peace mixed with our individual colours allows us to paint the most excellent of life paintings. Paintings, from which music can be heard. The kind of music, which has the power to pause the sniper.

And so one day, may pearl white be mixed into every individual's life painting. And may the colour of peace then reign in every nation. May there be piles of pearls—peaceful lives lived in excellence. Pearls found in water and brought up in beauty. An excellent life is like an excellent painting—a portrait painting of the value of life that is precious.

The United Nations Declaration of the Rights of the Child

The right to a name and nationality.

The right to affection, love, and understanding and to material security.

The right to adequate nutrition, housing and medical services.

The right to special care if handicapped, be it physically, mentally or socially.

The right to be among the first to receive protection and relief in all circumstances.

The right to be protected against all forms of neglect, cruelty and exploitation.

The right to full opportunity for play and recreation and equal opportunity to free and compulsory education, to enable the child to develop his individual abilities and to become a member of society.

The right to develop his full potential in conditions of freedom and dignity.

The right to be brought up in spirit of understanding, tolerance, friendship among people, peace, and universal brotherhood.

The right to enjoy these rights regardless of colour, race, sex, religion, political or other opinion, national or social origin , and property, birth or other status.

CPSIA information can be obtained at www.ICGtesting.com
Printed in the USA
LVOW08*2001210414

382609LV00001B/1/P